ON BORROWED TIME

PAUL OSBORN

ON
BORROWED
TIME

A Dramatization of the Novel by
Lawrence Edward Watkin

ALFRED · A · KNOPF
New York · 1938

ON BORROWED TIME

Presented by Dwight Deere Wiman at the Longacre Theatre in New York City beginning Thursday evening, February 3, 1938 with the following cast:

PUD	*played by*	PETER HOLDEN,
		PETER MINER,
		LAWRENCE ROBINSON
JULIAN NORTHRUP (GRAMPS)	" "	DUDLEY DIGGES
NELLIE (GRANNY)	" "	DOROTHY STICKNEY
MR. BRINK	" "	FRANK CONROY
MARCIA GILES	" "	PEGGY O'DONNELL
DEMETRIA RIFFLE	" "	JEAN ADAIR
A BOY	" "	DICKIE VAN PATTEN
WORKMEN	" "	ANDY ANDERSON ELWELL COBB NICK DENNIS
DR. EVANS	" "	CLYDE FRANKLIN
MR. PILBEAM	" "	RICHARD STERLING
MR. GRIMES	" "	LEW ECKELS
SHERIFF	" "	AL WEBSTER

Staged by JOSHUA LOGAN

Settings by JO MIELZINER

SYNOPSIS OF SCENES

ACT ONE

SCENE 1. *The living-room, afternoon.*

SCENE 2. *The living-room, afternoon, a week later.*

SCENE 3. *Granny's bedroom, a few minutes later.*

SCENE 4. *The tree, simultaneously with Scene 3.*

SCENE 5. *The tree, nearly dusk, a week later.*

ACT TWO

SCENE 1. *The tree, two hours later.*

SCENE 2. *The living-room, ten o'clock that night.*

SCENE 3. *The tree, dawn, the next morning.*

SCENE 4. *The tree, dusk, the same day.*

SCENE 5. *The tree, a few minutes later, the same day.*

SCENE 6. *The tree, later that night.*

ON BORROWED TIME

ACT ONE

SCENE I

The living-room. Late afternoon.
At Rise: GRAMPS *seated chair right of table, engraving.* PUD *crawls from under chair.*

PUD [*crawling out*]: You could write Pud on it afterwards.

GRAMPS: Yeh! I could write shikepoke on it too but I ain't goin' to.

PUD: What's shikepoke?

GRAMPS: A shikepoke's a bird.

PUD: Is it what you call the bird?

GRAMPS: Yup.
  [*Pause.*]

PUD [*climbs into* GRAMPS' *chair*]: If the watch fob belonged to the bird would you write shikepoke on it?

GRAMPS: Birds don't have watch fobs.

PUD: But if it did have one would you write shikepoke on it, Gramps?

GRAMPS: Expect I would.

PUD: Because it's what you call the bird, isn't it, Gramps?

GRAMPS: That's right, sonny.

[PUD *around back of chair. Pause.* GRAMPS *is busy.*]

PUD: Gramps, what do you call me?

GRAMPS: Eh? Oh, I call you all sorts of things—sonny, chummy—

PUD: No, no! What's the *name* you call me?

GRAMPS: Oh, Pud, you mean. Pud. That's what you look like. Pud.

PUD: It's what you call me, isn't it, Gramps?

GRAMPS: That's right, sonny.

PUD [*crosses to chair left*]: Then if the watch fob belongs to me and you call me Pud you ought to write Pud on it. If the shikepoke had a fob—

GRAMPS [*pause*]: Whoa there! I said I wasn't gonna write Pud on this here fob!

PUD: But Pud's my name.

GRAMPS: Your name is John Gilford Northrup. And that's what I'm gonna engrave on this here fob. John Gilford Northrup.

PUD: I like Pud better.

[*Climbs over chair left.*]

GRAMPS: Pud's too easy, P-U-D. John Gilford Northrup. And don't you forget it.

[*Pause.* GRAMPS *works.* PUD *rises, crosses right to desk.*]

PUD: Where's Mom gone today, Gramps?

GRAMPS: She's gone with your father.

PUD: Where did he go?

GRAMPS: Up to Gainesville to make a call.

PUD [*over chair right*]: Is somebody sick?

GRAMPS: Somebody's always sick, sonny.

[*Pause.*]

PUD: I'm going to be a doctor when I grow up.

GRAMPS: You bet you are. You're gonna be as good a doctor as your daddy.

PUD: Maybe better.

[*Crosses to* GRAMPS.]

GRAMPS: That's a stiff order, sonny. Your daddy's a A number one doctor.

PUD: What's A number one? [*Pause.*] What's A number one, Gramps?

GRAMPS: Oh, it's just A number one. There. Now, what do you think of that?

[PUD *looks at fob.*]

PUD: I guess it's all right, Gramps.

GRAMPS: What do you mean you guess it's all right?

PUD [*leans on arm of chair*]: Well, that G looks a little more like a C, I think.

GRAMPS: You do? Let's see.

[*Takes fob.*]

PUD: My name is John Gilford Northrup. Not John Cilford Northrup—

GRAMPS: I know that, boy, I know that. Well, guess that G does need a little more of a tail there. Yes sir, I guess it does. Thank you, boy.

[PUD *crosses to collection.*]

PUD: You're welcome, Gramps. Guess we better take a walk out to Milbaur Park one of these days, Gramps. We need some more stones for our collection.

GRAMPS [*reaching in his pocket.* PUD *crosses to* GRAMPS]: Oh, here's a bone I found yesterday down by the meatshop.

PUD: Is it a human bone, Gramps?

GRAMPS [*gives bone to* PUD]: Might be—

PUD: Looks pretty human to me, Gramps.

GRAMPS: Might be.

PUD [*crosses left to collection*]: It's a very fine specimen, anyway, Gramps. [*Pause.* PUD *goes over and
puts bone in collection and pulls out another object.*] This frog's gettin' kinda old, Gramps.
[*Crosses to table showing* GRAMPS *frog.*]

GRAMPS: Yep. Guess we'll have to throw that old frog
out in a few days.

PUD: It's a very fine specimen though, Gramps.

GRAMPS: We'll get another one.

[GRAMPS *gives* PUD *frog.* PUD *crosses to collection.
Pause. Puts label on bone.*]

PUD [*suddenly. Singing*]:

       Aunt Demetria is a pismire.

       Aunt Demetria is a pismire.

GRAMPS: Hey, there. Where did you hear that?

PUD: You told Granny she was.

GRAMPS: You mustn't use that word about your Aunt
Demetria.

PUD [*pointing at* GRAMPS]: *You* said she was a pismire.

GRAMPS: She *is* a pismire! She's the biggest pismire I
know. You know what a pismire is, sonny?

PUD: No.

[*Crosses to chair center, kneels on it.*]

GRAMPS: A pismire is one of the meanest of ants there

is. And your Aunt Demetria is a pismire. But you mustn't say it. It makes your Granny mad.

PUD: But why is Aunt Demetria so mean, Gramps?

GRAMPS: Born that way.

PUD: Why was she born that way?

GRAMPS: I'll tell you, boy, it's like this. Your other Gramps—

PUD: What, Gramps?

GRAMPS: I say when your other Gramps was alive . . .

PUD: What other Gramps?

GRAMPS: Your mom's father. Pshaw, boy, didn't you know you used to have another Gramps? Everybody has two Gramps.

PUD [*tearfully*]: But I don't want any other Gramps, Gramps. [GRAMPS *touches him.*] Did you have another Pud?

GRAMPS: No, 'course I didn't, boy. You're the only Pud I ever had.

PUD [*hits table*]: Then you're the only Gramps I ever had.

GRAMPS: All right, boy, all right. That other fellow —we'll call him your grand-father. Is that all right?

PUD: I guess so, Gramps.

GRAMPS: All right, then. So your grand-father had a whole lot of children. And the first one he had was your Aunt Demetria. That was a long time ago, when your grand-father was a young buck and didn't have no sense at all, so he didn't do a very good job of it. Botched it up all the way round. Then he had a lot more children to practice on and

the last one he had was your mother. Now, there
he did a real sweet job. Yes, sir, a pretty nigh per-
fect job.

PUD: But he sure made a mess out of Aunt Demetria.

GRAMPS: That's what I've been trying to tell you, boy.
[GRAMPS *takes bottle from pocket.*]

GRANNY [*off stage*]: Juleyun!

GRAMPS: Oh, hell!

PUD: Where is hell, Gramps?

GRAMPS: Where the woodbine twineth. [*He takes
sip from bottle.*] Don't you ever touch this, boy.

PUD: Give me some.

GRAMPS: No—

PUD: Just a little taste. . . .

GRAMPS: You wouldn't like 'er, boy!

PUD: Please, Gramps, please.

GRAMPS: Here then, teach yourself.
[*As* PUD *takes a drink* GRANNY *is heard calling again.*
PUD *spits it out.*]

GRANNY [*off stage*]: Juleyun!

PUD [*wipes mouth*]: Peeyew!

GRAMPS: Well, I warned you.

PUD [*gives bottle back*]: What do you drink it for,
Gramps?

GRAMPS: I drink it for my ches . . . because I li . . .
oh, because your Granny is yellin' at me and I got
to take that damn smelly dog out for a walk.

PUD: But I like the way Betty smells.

GRAMPS: You're welcome to it.
[*Hides bottle as* GRANNY *comes in with dog.*]

GRANNY [*crosses to table*]: When you two get together over some gimcrack you're as deaf as a post.

GRAMPS: Was you calling, Miss Nellie? Didn't hear
you.

GRANNY [*crosses right center*]: None so deaf as those
who don't want to hear.

GRAMPS: Well, what d'ye want?

GRANNY: I hollered loud enough to wake the dead.
That dog'll get caught short someday.

GRAMPS: Can't she find her own tree yet?

GRANNY: Julian! [*She nods toward* PUD.] Go with
your Grandpa, Betty.

GRAMPS [*takes leash*]: And I'll thank you not to claim
kin to me with that bitch!

GRANNY: Julian!
[*She points to* PUD.]

GRAMPS [*rises*]: Pshaw, that's what she is . . . no
more, no less than a bitch.

PUD [*singing, suddenly*]: A dog or a bitch, you never
know which.
[*They both look at* PUD.]

GRANNY: There you are!

GRAMPS: I never taught him that, Miss Nellie, I swear.

GRANNY [*crossing to desk*]: Turning your own grand-
son into a smutty mouth like yourself.

GRAMPS [*crossing center toward* GRANNY]: Honest, I
never taught him that, Miss Nellie.

GRANNY: That I should live to see the day . . . !

GRAMPS [*crossing to door*]: Oh, come along, Petunia.

GRANNY [*turning toward* GRAMPS]: And her name
isn't Petunia.

GRAMPS: All right, come along, sweet pea.

PUD [*rises, crosses up center to* GRAMPS]: I'll take her, Gramps. It's kinda *hot* for you to be out today.

GRAMPS: I guess you're right. It is. Thank you kindly. Go with your uncle, Betty.

[*He gives leash to* PUD.]

PUD: Am I her uncle?

GRAMPS [*looking toward* GRANNY]: Seems so.

GRANNY: Just walk her up toward the Browns, darling.

PUD: I know where her twalet is.

[PUD *and dog go off right.*]

GRANNY [*crossing to table left*]: That boy's gettin' to be the limit. You're not only making a smutty mouth out of him . . . [*She sits chair left.*] the first thing you know you'll be teaching him to smoke, I suppose. And even drink . . . and goodness knows what all.

GRAMPS [*sitting chair right of table*]: It'll be years yet before he can "What all"!

[*He lights pipe.*]

GRANNY: Julian!

GRAMPS: Oh, Miss Nellie.

GRANNY: He mimics everything you do. He hardly has a chance to see his own father. Jim's always so busy. First thing you know, that boy'll grow up and be just like you. Is that what you want?

GRAMPS: Nope. I want him to go further'n I have.

GRANNY: Then you better set him an example. You gotta stop swearin' and smokin' that smelly pipe. You never draw a breath that it ain't full of smokin'

and swearin'. You better change your ways, Julian
Northrup. If you don't, I'm gonna talk to Jim and
Susan about sending Pud away to school.

GRAMPS: Send him away to school? At his age?

GRANNY: It'd be better for him than being around you
so much.

GRAMPS: There ain't no school what'd take him. He's
too little.

GRANNY: Yes, there is. Demetria knows a school
in . . .

GRAMPS: Demetria! By God, I might have known
she was at the bottom of this. [GRANNY *looks at
him.*] Old bird-stuffer!

GRANNY: Demetria's a fine, Christian woman and I
won't hear a word against her.

GRAMPS: She's a bird-stuffer!

GRANNY: She's no such thing.

GRAMPS: Oh, Miss Nellie—I don't see why you're always sticking up for Demmie. She's a bird-stuffer
and you know it.

GRANNY: Demmie may have her faults but she's a God-
fearing woman. She's warned Susan time and time
again how you're poisoning Pud's mind, and now
she's found this nice boarding-school run by a Baptist woman.

GRAMPS: Baptist woman! By God, Pud's not goin' to
no school run by a Baptist woman.

GRANNY: Then you better change your ways, Julian
Northup. You are a bad influence on the boy and
it's gotta be stopped. It's gotta be. . . . [*She
belches sharply.*] There! Now I've got that gas

started again. Every time I get excited it starts rumbling and rumbling.

GRAMPS: Well, you'd better not get excited, then. [*He rises, crosses to window, looking at fob.*]

GRANNY: It won't be long before I'm flat on my back for good now. [*Pause. She looks at* GRAMPS.] What is a bird-stuffer, Julian?

GRAMPS: It's just a bird-stuffer.

GRANNY: But it must *mean* something.

GRAMPS: Nope. It don't. Adam saw a dog and it looked like a dog and he called it a dog. I saw Demmie, she looked like a bird-stuffer and I called her a bird-stuffer, so she is a bird-stuffer. [*Pause.*]

GRANNY: Sultry today, ain't it?

GRAMPS: Hotter'n a bull mink in matin' season.

GRANNY: That I don't know about. [GRAMPS *laughs. Pause.*] Guess we'll have another shower. Hope it won't spoil Susan's day. She so seldom goes with Jim on a case.

GRAMPS [*crossing to window*]: What did she go for today?

GRANNY: For the pleasure of bein' with him. I suppose you can't understand a thing like that. You always used to go off by yourself . . . though like enough there was someone waitin' around the corner.

GRAMPS [*looking out the window*]: Here comes someone around the corner now. Umhum!

GRANNY: Who is it?

GRAMPS: The Widow Tritt.

GRANNY [*rises, crosses right to* GRAMPS]: That hussy! Demmie says she ought to be run outa town.

GRAMPS: Not a bad looking woman, considering all she's been through. Five, ain't it?

GRANNY: Demmie says she makes advances to every man she meets.

GRAMPS: Widows always have somethin' about them. She kin put her shoes under my bed anytime she wants to.

GRANNY: Just as well you're eighty odd. Even then, I don't know. [*She crosses a step or two toward* GRAMPS. *Looks out of window also. He catches her at it.*] Well, don't stand there in the window staring at her. You don't know her, do you?

GRAMPS: Sure wish I did.

GRANNY: Julian!

[*She crosses to chair left.*]

GRAMPS [*singing*]:
She remained up in the mountains,
She remained up in the mountains,
Remained up in the mountains all that night.

GRANNY: And I wish you wouldn't sing that lascivious song.

VOICE [*off stage*]: Good afternoon, Mr. Northrup.

GRAMPS: Hello there, Mrs. Tritt.

GRANNY: Well, I never.

VOICE: 'Fraid it's goin' to rain.

GRAMPS: Yup, looks like it.

VOICE: I've got to hurry. Mustn't be caught short.

[*Pause.* GRANNY *stands staring at* GRAMPS. *He looks at her sheepishly.*]

GRAMPS: Sure mustn't. [*Pause. He turns and looks at* GRANNY.] Well, what're you standin' there like a hitchin' post for?

GRANNY: And you don't know the Widow Tritt.

GRAMPS [*crossing to* GRANNY]: Miss Nellie, I swear to you I never . . .

GRANNY: Never what?

GRAMPS: What you're insinuating. I petted her dog once.

GRANNY: Oh, you petted her dog. . . .

GRAMPS: I didn't even know it was her dog. She was in the grocery store and . . . Oh, you needn't pretend to think I ever had . . .

GRANNY [*crossing center*]: Never mind, Julian. And I think I'll go upstairs now.

GRAMPS [*starts to kiss her*]: Aw, Miss Nellie!

GRANNY: I'm not jealous. I just don't feel very well. [*She goes upstairs.*]

GRAMPS [*crossing back of chair right of table*]: All right, Miss Nellie. I'll come up and lie down, too, soon as Pud comes in. I'm feeling kind of tired myself. [*He looks after* GRANNY. *Then looks at window. Begins to sing, as he crosses around chair.*] Her life is beer and skittles And she is eating fancy vittles And them West Virginia . . . [MR. BRINK *appears.* GRAMPS *is striken with pain. Falls into chair right of table.*]

BRINK: Mr. Julian Northrup, I believe?

GRAMPS: What's that? I didn't catch it.

BRINK [*crossing down center*]: Most people don't hear me the first time.

GRAMPS: How in blazes could I hear you if I was asleep?

BRINK: Are you sure you were—asleep?

GRAMPS: Guess I musta drowsed off. Felt kind of tired all of a sudden. Who are you? What d'ye want?

BRINK: I request that you come with me.

GRAMPS: Where yuh goin'?

BRINK: Where the woodbine twineth.

GRAMPS: Where the wood . . . ? *I* just said that. I made it up. It's what yuh say to a child. *I* ain't no child.

BRINK: Aren't you?

GRAMPS: No, I'm not. Say, look here, who the hell are you?

BRINK: You may call me Mr. Brink.

GRAMPS: Well, look here, Mr. Brink, I don't like you. I wouldn't go with you to a rat fight, so now you know.

BRINK: I'm sorry.

GRAMPS: I don't like the way you snuck up here. I don't like the way you talk. [*He leans over to pick up fob and instrument which fell from his hands.*]

BRINK: I'm afraid that will have to be as it may be.

GRAMPS: Oh, you are! Well, you better . . . [*Rises.*] . . . get out of here right awa . . .

[*He becomes suddenly weak and sits, bewildered.*]

BRINK [*crossing closer to him*]: You see. It's time for you to come with me.

GRAMPS: No . . . no. . . . It ain't. I ain't goin' no-where. I'm goin' to stay right here. I'm waitin' for Pud. [*He gets stronger. Rises, waves hands.*] By God, you get the hell out of here! You git off my son's property! You git the hell . . .

[GRANNY's *voice off stage stops him.* BRINK *turns swiftly and leaves.* GRAMPS *turns toward* GRANNY's *voice, then turns back to door.*]

GRANNY [*off stage.*]: Julian!

GRAMPS [*turning back to door*]: You git the . . .
[*He discovers* MR. BRINK *has disappeared and is bewildered.*] Well, I'll be . . .
[*Crosses to chair right of table and sits.*]

GRANNY [*comes down on stairs*]: Who you shoutin' at that way?

GRAMPS: Well, I . . . there was a feller here. . . .

GRANNY: Well, where is he?

GRAMPS: He's gone now.

GRANNY: What did he want?

GRAMPS: I don't rightly know, Miss Nellie. I . . .

GRANNY: You better come upstairs out of that hot room, Julian.
[*She goes off.*]

GRAMPS: Yes, I guess I better had.
[PUD *comes in from porch with* BETTY.]

PUD: Gramps, who was that mans?

GRAMPS: You seen him, did you, son?

PUD: Sure. He was coming down the walk. Who was he?

GRAMPS: I don't rightly know who he was.

PUD: What did he want?

GRAMPS: He wanted me to go with him.

PUD: Where?

GRAMPS: Where the woodbine twineth.

PUD: Oh! You mean, Hell.

GRAMPS [*rising*]: By golly, boy, we better both go
upstairs out of this hot room.
[*They go upstairs.*]

CURTAIN

SCENE II

The living-room. Late afternoon. A week later.
AT RISE: PUD *is reading on floor.* GRAMPS *is writ-*
ing at desk. GRANNY *is knitting.* MARCIA *is handing*
GRANNY *a drink.*

GRANNY [*seated in chair right of table*]: Thank you,
Marcy. I'll just keep it here till I need it.
[*Wipes eyes with mourning handkerchief.*]

MARCIA: How are you feeling, Mrs. Northup?

GRANNY: Won't be long before I'm flat on my back
for good, now.

MARCIA [*patting* GRANNY'S *shoulder*]: Oh, you got
years and years yet, Mrs. Northrup.
[MARCIA *crosses to bookcase up right and straight-*
ens it.]

GRANNY: Don't know as I want years and years yet.

GRAMPS: Anyways, where the hell's some more ink?

MARCIA [*crossing down to desk*]: Here's some, Mr. Northrup.

GRAMPS: Oh, thank ye, Marcy. How did we ever find things before you came to live with us?

[MARCIA *smiles and returns to bookcase. Pause.* GRAMPS *writes.* GRANNY *knits.*]

PUD [*suddenly*]: Granny, why do they put dead peoples in coffings?

GRANNY: Oh, Pud!

[*She buries her face in her hands, crying suddenly.*]

GRAMPS: There, there, Miss Nellie! [*Rises and crosses to her.*] Now, don't talk about that any more, boy.

PUD: But why do they, Gramps?

MARCIA [*going down to and kneeling beside* PUD]: 'Cause that's the way you take care of 'em. Now, read your story, Pud.

[GRAMPS *looks at* GRANNY. PUD *is quiet.*]

GRAMPS: That's all right, Miss Nellie. That's all right.

GRANNY [*looking up at him*]: I don't know—I'm just so tired, Julian.

GRAMPS: 'Course you are. Now, everything's all right, Miss Nellie.

[*He kisses her on the forehead and crosses to desk.*]

PUD: Is it comfable in a coffing?

GRAMPS: Yes, boy, very comfortable in a coffin.

PUD: As comfable as my bed?

GRAMPS [*sitting at desk*]: Sure, sure. 'Course it is. As comfortable as your bed. [*Motioning to book on floor.*] Now read your damn story.

[*Pause.* GRANNY *gets hold of herself.*]

GRANNY: It's very comfortable in a coffin, Pud.

PUD [*suddenly. Rises*]: My mamma and papa are in coffings. They put them in the ground like this— [*He crosses to* GRANNY *to illustrate.*] You may lower now. Dear Lord, we commend to thy tender—

GRAMPS [*turning quickly*]: Don't, Pud. Don't. I told you—

GRANNY [*taking* PUD *in her arms*]: That's all right, Julian.—Yes, dear, your mamma and papa are both very comfortable.

PUD: My papa was a brave man, wasn't he?

GRANNY: Yes, he was, dear—very brave.

PUD: He turned his automobile right off the road so he wouldn't hurt a little boy just like me.

GRANNY: That's right, darling.

PUD [*as though repeating a lesson*]: But I must never forget that my dear mamma and papa were taken from me and I will never, never have any others. I'm a—orphan.

GRAMPS [*quickly*]: Who told you that?

PUD [*turning to* GRAMPS]: Aunt Demetria.

GRAMPS [*roaring and pointing to* GRANNY]: There! That damned old—!

GRANNY: Julian!

GRAMPS: Telling things like that to the boy! By God, if that God-damned old hellion—

GRANNY: Julian! If you swear any more like that in front of—

GRAMPS: It's enough to make a preacher swear.

PUD: I'm going to swear when I'm nine.

GRAMPS [*shaking his finger*]: Ah— Ah—

PUD [*crossing to* GRAMPS]: But you said I could, Gramps.

[GRAMPS *motions violently for* PUD *to go back to his book.* PUD *sits.*]

GRANNY [*angrily*]: There! Did you tell that boy he could . . . Did you tell that boy he could . . . [*She belches sharply.*] Whoops, there it goes again! Never know when it's coming. [*She drinks.* GRAMPS *writes. Pause.*] Who you writin' to, anyway, Julian?

GRAMPS: Reverend Murdock. Looked pretty shabby when he was preachin' that funeral sermon. I guess preachin' don't pay what it used to.

[*Pause.* GRAMPS *writes.*]

GRANNY: What are you writin' him for?

GRAMPS: Goin' to send him a check for $50.00. [*Turning to* GRANNY.] Now, that's a good deed, ain't it, even if I do say so myself?

GRANNY: Good deeds and leadin' a Christian life is two different things.

PUD [*rising to his knees, excited*]: Oh, Gramps, if you do a good deed, you can make a wish and it'll come true.

GRAMPS [*back at desk*]: What's that?

PUD: If you do a good deed, you can make a wish and it'll come true.

GRAMPS: That so, boy?

PUD: That's what my book says.

GRAMPS: Must be so then.

PUD [*very excited*]: So make a wish, Gramps, make a wish, make a wish.

GRAMPS: All right, boy, soon's I think of a good one. [*Pause. He turns to* GRANNY.] Listen, Miss Nellie, how does this sound?

"Dear Reverend Murdock: Enclosed is a check for $50.00, for which please kindly send me one copy of the sermon you preached at the funeral of my son, James Northrup, M.D., and his wife, Susan. If you don't have it down on paper, maybe you wouldn't mind writing out the jist of the thing which I thought was very good and proper and appropriate to the occasion. I hope the enclosed check will compensate in some part for the trouble this will make you.

Yours truly,
Julian Northrup."

Now, you don't think he'd take offense at that, do you?

GRANNY: I don't think so, Julian.

GRAMPS [*turning back to desk*]: No. Don't want to offend the old bastard.

GRANNY [*rising*]: Julian!

GRAMPS: Sorry, Miss Nellie. Take it back. Forgot. [*Pause.*]

PUD [*suddenly rising and unbuttoning pants*]: I'm going to the twalet.

GRANNY: What!

PUD: I'm going to the twalet.

GRANNY: Well, you don't have to tell the neighbors about it. When you have to go, just get up quietly and go.

GRAMPS: Just say you have to wash your hands, boy.

PUD [*crossing to* GRAMPS]: But I don't have to wash my hands.

GRAMPS: Don't make no difference. That's what you say. Etiquette. [*Pause.*] Matter of fact my hands feels kinda dirty, too, but I guess I'll wait until they're a little dirtier.

GRANNY: Go along, Pud! [PUD *runs upstairs.* GRANNY *puts her knitting on the table and turns back to* GRAMPS, *shaking her head disapprovingly.*] 'Twasn't an accident!

GRAMPS: What's that?

GRANNY: 'Twasn't an accident that killed Jim and Susan.

GRAMPS [*turning to her*]: Sure, of course it was, Miss Nellie—they turned over in their car.

GRANNY: God took Jim and Susan, Julian.

GRAMPS: Oh. Oh!

[*Goes back to his writing.*]

GRANNY: As a warnin' to us. Julian, I heard the voice of God at the funeral. I was sittin' there durin' the hymn, askin' myself why this cross had been put upon us. What had we done that was bad? And suddenly it came to me. It was you!

GRAMPS [*turning quickly*]: Me?

GRANNY: You and me both, Julian.

GRAMPS: Well, what've we been doin' that's bad, Miss Nellie? I can't think of nothin'. Less you been up to somethin'.

GRANNY: I have, Julian. I've been closing my eyes to the way you've been ruinin' Pud. [*She rises and goes to* GRAMPS *at desk.*] We can't raise a little boy,

Julian—all by ourselves—we're too old.

GRAMPS: Why, sure we can, Miss Nellie—same way we raised Jim. I'll keep teaching him to cuss and you'll keep teaching him not to. He'll turn out pretty good, you'll see.

GRANNY [*turning away*]: We gotta find some other way to raise that boy.

GRAMPS: Ain't nobody goin' to raise that boy but us!

GRANNY [*turning to him*]: Julian, the Lord said . . .

GRAMPS: The Lord be blowed— You heard the voice of Demetria.

GRANNY [*crosses left*]: No, it 'twasn't. It was the Lord's!

GRAMPS: It was Demetria's!

GRANNY: Julian Northrup, I guess I know the difference between the Lord's voice and Demetria Riffle's. [PUD *enters from stairs, trying to fasten his pants.*]

PUD: I've had my fun and now I'm done.

GRANNY: What!

PUD [*coming center*]: I've had my fun and now I'm done.

GRANNY: You've had . . . [*Turning toward* GRAMPS.] There you are!

GRAMPS: Never taught him that, Miss Nellie.

GRANNY: Julian.

GRAMPS: I never taught him that.

GRANNY: You're a liar, Julian Northrup.

GRAMPS: Well, maybe I am.
    [PUD *goes to* GRAMPS *and backs up toward him.*]

PUD [*pointing to his pants*]: Back door's undone.

GRAMPS [*pushes him*]: Go to your Granny.

[PUD *crosses to* GRANNY.]

GRANNY [*sits*]: Yes, come here, darling. I'll help you.
  [*Together they fasten the pants.*] Get you all but-
  toned up nice and tight. [*She tries to kiss him.*]
  Got a nice kiss for Granny? [PUD *struggles away.*]
  What's the matter, darling?

PUD: I've had too much ladies' arms around me lately.

GRANNY: Too *many* arms.

PUD [*crosses left to* GRAMPS]: Too many arms. I'd
  like to have none arms around me for a while.

GRANNY: Oh, very well.
  [*She goes back to her knitting.*]

GRAMPS [*taking hold of* PUD]: You hadn't ought to
  say things like that to your Granny. If she wants to
  give you a kiss now and then, just let her do it.

PUD: She kisses awful wet.

GRAMPS: What the hell, that don't cut no ice. . . .
  [PUD *crosses to above desk.*] And I don't want to
  ever see you smoke or say dirty things . . . and,
  above all . . . [*Shakes his finger at* PUD.] . . . I
  don't ever want to hear you swear. . . .
  [*Turns and looks triumphantly at* GRANNY. PUD, *at
  this point, has turned and is staring out of the window right.*]

PUD: Gramps, Gramps, somebody's stealing the apples again.

GRAMPS: God-damn it to hell. Where is he?
  [*Rises.*]

PUD [*getting into chair*]: He's up the tree.

GRAMPS [*shouting out the window*]: Hey, you damn
  young shikepoke. I'm comin' out there and get

you. You wait right there.

PUD: Hurry, Gramps, he's coming down.

GRAMPS: You stay up there. I'm goin' to give you such a tannin'—

PUD: He's gettin' away, Gramps.

GRAMPS [*crossing closer to window*]: Hey, there— wait. . . .

PUD [*turning around from window*]: Oh, Gramps, he got away. He didn't wait.

GRAMPS [*snapping fingers*]: Oh, hell—

GRANNY [*laughs*]: Heh! Heh!

GRAMPS [*coming center*]: I swear I wish that anyone who climbed that tree would have to stay up there until I let him down.

PUD [*excitedly crossing to* GRAMPS]: Gramps, you made a wish!

GRAMPS: Huh?

PUD: A wish! You wished anyone who climbed that tree would have to stay there until you let him down.

GRAMPS [*crosses to desk, picks up letter*]: A lot of good it'll do me.

PUD [*jumps around excitedly*]: Gee, I bet we catch one of those bad boys up there and we can keep him up there for a hundred years. Maybe for a million years. Maybe . . .

[PUD *stops suddenly and becomes very quiet, staring at the door.* DEMETRIA *enters, takes off hat, puts it on hat-rack.*]

GRANNY [*following* PUD's *eyes*]: Oh, hello, Demmie.

GRAMPS: Oh, hell.

GRANNY: Come right in.

DEMETRIA [*crossing center, taking* PUD *in arms*]: Poor little lambie, what's the matter? Is he still thinking of his mamma and papa?

GRAMPS: Leave that boy alone, for God's sake!

GRANNY: Julian!

DEMETRIA: Well!

PUD [*struggling*]: Let me go!

DEMETRIA: There, there, lambie, your Aunt Demetria understands. [*She ruffles* PUD's *hair. He straightens it with a defiant gesture.*] You must be a brave boy, boy. God has taken . . .

GRAMPS: Leave that boy alone, I say.

DEMETRIA: Would you deny the child Christian comfort, his parents hardly cold in their graves . . . ? [PUD *runs to* GRAMPS, *crying.*]

GRAMPS [*clasping* PUD]: To hell with Christian comfort, you old . . .

DEMETRIA: Come here, Pud.

PUD: I hate you!

GRAMPS: Now you know.

DEMETRIA: Come here to me, Pud.

GRAMPS: Like hell he will!

PUD: Like hell I will!

DEMETRIA [*to* GRANNY]: See! See! [*To* GRAMPS.] You whited sepulchre!

GRAMPS: What! Whited sepulch . . . You—whore of Babylon! You—
[*He crosses to door center, spluttering.*]

PUD [*following*]: You—pismire!

GRAMPS [*taking his hand*]: That's right, boy. Come

along. Let's get out of this company.
[*They go out by the porch, leaving* DEMETRIA *and* GRANNY *speechless.*]

DEMETRIA: You heard it, Nellie.

GRANNY: I never thought I'd live to—

DEMETRIA [*coming down right*]: You heard what he called me! He called me . . .

GRANNY: I know. Revelations 17:5. Don't say it, Demmie.

DEMETRIA [*sitting at desk*]: Of course, I know I'm a nobody, Nellie. Maybe I'm no better than some folks say I am. But I'm certainly not a whor—

GRANNY: Of course you're not, Demmie. I don't know what Julian was thinking of.

DEMETRIA: And he said it right in front of that sweet little boy. But, then, of course, it's none of my business.

GRANNY [*sitting in chair left of table*]: Of course it's your business.

DEMETRIA: No. I guess I better stay home after this. I'm a downright nuisance.

GRANNY: You're not. You're a dear, sweet, Christian woman and you shouldn't always be runnin' yourself down. You're the only God-fearing woman . . . Well! . . . Maybe that's what the voice of God meant.

DEMETRIA: What?

GRANNY: I wonder if you shouldn't bring Pud up?

DEMETRIA: Me?

GRANNY: Your own sister's child. And you could bring him up the way God wants him to be brought up. Maybe that's what God meant.

DEMETRIA: Well, Nellie, I've thought about it. [*Crossing to chair right of table.*] But I couldn't afford to give Pud all the things he's been used to. That is, unless Jim left a will—or something like that.

GRANNY: Well, he did, Demmie. He left a will.

DEMETRIA [*sits*]: Well, think of that. And how m . . . that is . . . well, is the little lambie well taken care of?

GRANNY: Yes, Demmie. Jim left fifty-five thousand dollars.

DEMETRIA: Fifty-five thou . . . ! Dear little lambie. . . . Well, Nellie, maybe you're right.

GRANNY: About what—?

DEMETRIA [*rises, crosses center*]: Maybe I should adopt Pud.

GRANNY: Adopt him . . . ?

DEMETRIA: I mean if he has fifty-five thousand dollars, I could give him some of the things he's been used to.

GRANNY: Yes, but adopt him . . . I didn't exactly mean . . . well, you wouldn't really have to adopt him, would you, Demmie? I just thought he'd sort of live over there with you and see Julian in the afternoons maybe and you could kind of . . . No. I guess not, Demmie. . . . I mean, Julian and I better . . .

DEMETRIA: I see. You mean you are going to go on letting Julian bring Pud up like a heathen.

GRANNY: Oh, I don't know what to do, Demmie. I'm so tired.

[MARCIA *enters from hallway, with glass of soda water, crosses down to table.*]

MARCIA: Would you like some more soda, Mrs. Northrup?

GRANNY: Yes, I would, Marcy. Still feel a little rumbly down there.

MARCIA: Good afternoon, Miss Riffle.

DEMETRIA [*crossing right. Coldly*]: Good afternoon. [MARCIA *goes out through porch, bewildered.* DEMETRIA *crosses back to table.*] You don't mean to tell me you've got that Marcia Giles in this house.

GRANNY: She came in to help us after the funeral. Why? Good straight-forward girl, isn't she?

DEMETRIA: Well, her and that young Bill Murdock, Reverend Murdock's son . . .

GRANNY: Well, yes, Demmie . . . what about them?

DEMETRIA: Carrying on! Just as brazen as you please! [GRAMPS *enters on to porch, carrying dead frog.*] And you're allowing a person like that to be around where Pud is. Nellie Northrup!

GRANNY [*rises*]: But I didn't know about it, Demmie.

DEMETRIA: You could've asked me.

[GRAMPS *comes in from porch, whistling.*]

GRAMPS [*coming center to* DEMETRIA]: Dead frog! Brand new. Beautiful specimen. Pud just found it. [*He thrusts frog into* DEMETRIA's *face. She reacts.* GRAMPS *continues toward collection down right.*]

DEMETRIA: How perfectly disgusting!

GRAMPS [*at collection*]: Oh, don't feel that way, Demmie. We're gonna put *you* right up there next to him some day.

GRANNY: Julian!

[GRAMPS *crosses to desk right and picks up mushroom book.*]

GRAMPS: In a hurry, Miss Nellie. Pud's waitin' for me under the barn. He just found a new mushroom. [*He thumbs through the book.*] Think we got a Pleaurotus Ostreatus!

GRANNY [*crossing to right of table*]: Julian, be careful. That may be a toadstool!

GRAMPS [*crossing to door and still thumbing through book*]: Well, that's what we're gonna find out.

DEMETRIA [*back of table. Whispering to* GRANNY]: Marcia!

GRANNY [*moving center*]: Julian, wait a minute.

GRAMPS [*going to her*]: What is it, Miss Nellie?

GRANNY: It's Marcia. I'm afraid we'll have to get rid of her. It seems she's carrying on with young Bill Murdock.

GRAMPS: Bill Murdock? Good. Nice boy, Bill.

DEMETRIA [*moving around left of table*]: And you're willing to have that kind of girl in your own home?

GRAMPS: What do you mean—that kind of a girl?

DEMETRIA: Why, she's nothing more than a common, little—

GRAMPS: You're a God-damned liar!

GRANNY: Don't you talk that way to Demmie, Julian. We don't know anything about Marcia.

GRAMPS: I know about her. Knew she was a nice girl the minute I saw her.

GRANNY: Demmie knows what she's talking about.

GRAMPS [*to* DEMETRIA]: What do you know? Just tell me one thing!

DEMETRIA [*crosses to chair right of table*]: All right. I saw them—right in the park.

GRAMPS: And what were they doin'? Right in the park.

DEMETRIA: Kissin'! Kissin'—like you never saw. Fair make your blood boil. If they carry on like that in public, what must they do when they're alone?

GRANNY: Well, but Demmie—maybe they just kiss.

GRAMPS: Ye Gods—*that makes me mad!* That makes me so God-damned mad . . .

GRANNY: Julian Northrup, you stop your swearing! You stop your swearing!

GRAMPS: Miss Nellie, if you listen to another word this old hellion says you're just a plain fool!

GRANNY [*shakes finger at* GRAMPS]: Don't you call me a fool, Julian Northrup, don't you call me a fool!

GRAMPS [*roaring louder*]: I'm disappointed in you, Miss Nellie, I'm disappointed in you!

GRANNY [*sinks weakly into chair right of table*]: Oh, dear! Oh, dear.

DEMETRIA: There, now. You've tired yourself all out.

GRANNY [*rising*]: I guess you'd better help me to my room, Demmie. I guess I better lie down, now.

GRAMPS [*pushing* DEMETRIA]: Stand back, you. I'll help you, Miss Nellie.

[DEMETRIA *picks up* GRANNY's *knitting from table*.]

GRANNY [*facing him*]: No, Julian Northrup, I only

want them to help me that knows how to help me.
[DEMETRIA *looks at* GRAMPS *triumphantly as they
go out.*]

DEMETRIA: I never should have told you about Marcia.
It's all my fault.

GRANNY: You did just right, Demmie, you did just
right.
[*They are out of sight up the stairs.* GRAMPS *stands
watching them off, fuming.*]

GRAMPS: Damned old hellion! Even makes me fight
with Miss Nellie!
[MARCIA *enters from porch.*]

MARCIA: Mr. Northrup, Pud's yelling for you—
[*Starts out.*]

GRAMPS [*at desk. Shouts at her*]: Come here. What
the devil do you mean by kissing men in the park?

MARCIA [*coming to him, frightened*]: What?

GRAMPS: Don't you know it's a sin for a girl to kiss
men in the park?

MARCIA: But—but I didn't—I didn't kiss men in the
park! I only kissed one man in the park.

GRAMPS: What'd you kiss him in the park for?

MARCIA [*nearly crying*]: Because we were in the park
and . . .

GRAMPS: Well, next time you bring him up here and
kiss him!

MARCIA: Wh-what?

GRAMPS: I say, you bring that Bill Murdock up here
and kiss him. 'Stime we had a little kissin' in this
house again. How the hell's Pud gonna learn about
kissin' if he don't never see any of it?

MARCIA: Oh, Mr. Northrup!
[*She throws her arms around* GRAMPS *and begins to cry.*]

GRAMPS [*softer*]: There, there, Marcy. You in love with him?

MARCIA: Yes, oh, yes. We've been engaged all summer now.

GRAMPS: Yep. I thought I recognized the symptoms.

MARCIA: Bill's only got one more year at Law School and then we're gonna be married. He took highest honors in his class last year.

GRAMPS: Well, you just tell that to Miss Nellie and everything'll be all right. And the next time you and Bill meet Demetria in the park you make Bill give you a big smacker right in front of her. Just like this.
[*He kisses her.*]

MARCIA: Oh, did Miss Riffle tell you? That's why she . . .

DEMETRIA [*off stage*]: Marcia!

MARCIA [*turning center*]: Yes, Miss Riffle.

DEMETRIA [*off stage*]: Mrs. Northrup wants you to make her a cup of tea. And she has something to say to you.

MARCIA [*looks at* GRAMPS]: All right, Miss Riffle.

GRAMPS [*going to her*]: You just tell Miss Nellie that you and Bill are engaged and that Bill got highest honors in his class.

MARCIA: All right. [*Pause.* MARCIA *turns.*] Mr. Northrup.

GRAMPS: Huh?

MARCIA: Bill only got next to highest honors in his class.

[PUD *enters from porch and stands in doorway.*]

GRAMPS: Tell her he got next to highest honors. Next to highest's good enough—God-damn it. [MARCIA *smiles at him and goes out left.* GRAMPS *stands looking after her, chuckling.*] Real sweet girl, Marcy.

PUD [*looking after* MARCIA]: Gee, I wish Granny would knit two bumps on the front of my sweater the way Marcy's got on hers.

GRAMPS [*turns to* PUD]: What? Hey there, you! None of that from you, young man. Not that there ain't something in what you say.

[*He drags* PUD *off by ear.*]

CURTAIN

SCENE III

GRANNY'S *bedroom, directly above living-room. It is an old-fashioned room, with sloping, attic ceiling. Window right is directly above window in living-room. Door center opens on to hallway. A large, dark closet is left.*

Action is simultaneous with end of Scene 2.

AT RISE: GRANNY *is in bed.* DEMETRIA *is straightening bed covers.*

GRANNY: He can't call me a fool, Demmie. He can't say he's disappointed in me.

DEMETRIA: I don't see why you stand for it, Nellie. [*Hands* GRANNY *her knitting from bed table left.*] Now, here's your knitting. How's your gas?

GRANNY: Feels a little quieter, I guess. 'Course you can't trust it. Sneaks up on you so.

DEMETRIA: Are you going to speak to Marcia?

GRANNY: Well, I don't know—if you just saw them kissin'.

DEMETRIA: Nellie!

GRANNY: All right, Demmie. Call to her. Ask her to make me a cup of tea.

[DEMETRIA *goes to door and calls.* GRANNY *knits.*]

DEMETRIA: Marcia!

MARCIA [*off stage*]: Yes, Miss Riffle.

DEMETRIA: Mrs. Northrup wants you to make her a cup of tea and she has something to say to you.

MARCIA [*off stage*]: All right, Miss Riffle.

[DEMETRIA *comes back, picks up coverlet from chair left.*]

GRANNY: I hate to do it. She needs the money so bad.

DEMETRIA: There are some things more important than money, Nellie.

GRANNY: Well, maybe you're right. There. I'll just finish this mitten. I was makin' 'em for Jim but Julian can use 'em. And after my cup of tea, think I could drop off for a spell.

DEMETRIA: Just what you should do, Nellie.

[DEMETRIA *crosses right and lights lamp on bed table right.*]

GRANNY: Feel kinda funny. [*Pause.* DEMETRIA *glances out window right; sits in chair right of bed.*] He don't mean all the things he says. He's just a rough-spoken man is all.

DEMETRIA [*ties her shoe*]: Who? Julian?

GRANNY: And he ain't a blasphemer either—not exactly. He never sneers at religion. He just don't have no interest in it.

DEMETRIA: Amounts to the same thing.

GRANNY [*reflectively*]: Good-looking man too, in his day.

DEMETRIA: Julian?

GRANNY: Umm. I remember him at a party when the old century went out. Handsome as anything. Everybody was after him.

DEMETRIA [*fixing her gloves*]: I guess he's had plenty in his day.

GRANNY: Not since we've been married he ain't.

DEMETRIA: Well, I didn't say that, Nellie.

GRANNY: Not any I know about, anyways. Julian's always been a pretty good . . . [*Pause.*] Demmie, will you go down and ask Julian to step up here for a minute? I want to see him.

DEMETRIA: Now, Nellie, you're not goin' to forgive him.

GRANNY: I'm not goin' to exactly forgive him, Demmie. I just want to tell him somethin'.

[GRANNY *gets sleepy and dozes off.*]

DEMETRIA: All right, I'll go in a minute or two. [*Sees* GRANNY *is dozing.*] Nellie dear, do you think I should take Pud's things over with me now?

GRANNY [*sleepily*]: Pud's things?

DEMETRIA [*lulling her with her voice*]: Yes. And in

the morning, I'll go down to Mr. Pilbeam's and have the papers drawn up for you to sign—about the will and the adoption—and all. . . .

GRANNY [*waking with a start*]: Now, see here, Demmie—I didn't say anything about your adoptin' Pud. You're trying to put words in my mouth. I don't like the way you're actin', Demmie.

DEMETRIA: Nellie Northrup, you said five minutes ago that I should bring Pud up.

GRANNY: I just wondered about it, Demmie.

DEMETRIA: You said it, Nellie.

GRANNY: If I did, I was wrong. I can see that now. . . . I don't like the way you're actin', Demmie. [*She falls back, weakly.*] Oh, dear.

DEMETRIA [*rises*]: There, now, Nellie, don't think about it any more, now.

GRANNY: Ask Julian to come up, Demmie. I want to see him.

DEMETRIA [*pointing down, out of window*]: There! There's a boy going up that apple tree!

GRANNY: Apples nice and ripe now.

DEMETRIA: Those nasty brats deserve a good whipping. Stealing other people's property!

GRANNY: Julian never catches 'em. He starts bellowin' to give 'em plenty of time to get away.

DEMETRIA: Well, I bet I can catch 'em! There! He's just gone up the tree. I can just catch him nicely! [*She hurries to the door.*] Nasty little thief. . . . [*Exits.*]

GRANNY: And don't forget to tell Julian to step up a minute. . . .

[DEMETRIA *is already out of the room.* GRANNY *hums, tries to knit, then drowses off. Pause.* MARCIA *enters with tea tray.*]

MARCIA: Here's your tea, Mrs. Northrup.

GRANNY [*faintly*]: Oh, just set it down, Marcy.

MARCIA [*frightened*]: Is there anything wrong, Mrs. Northrup?

GRANNY: Wrong? No, there's nothing wrong, Marcy. I'm just kind of tired. I'm goin' to go to sleep in a minute. . . . Now, let me see, there was somethin' I was supposed to talk to you about! Now, what was it? . . . Well, there, I've forgotten. Couldn't have been very important. [*Pause.*] Marcy!

MARCIA: Yes, Mrs. Northrup?

GRANNY [*takes* MARCIA's *hand*]: Marcy—you just see that Julian always has his pipe. Will you do that?

MARCIA [*bewildered*]: Yes, Mrs. Northrup.

GRANNY: You're a good girl, Marcy. Now, go on back to whatever you're doin'.

[MARCIA *goes out, puzzled.* GRANNY *tries to knit again. Has difficulty in seeing. Drowses off again.* BRINK *appears from closet left.*]

BRINK [*approaching bed*]: Don't you think you have done enough?

GRANNY [*waking*]: That you, Julian?

BRINK: No, not Julian.

GRANNY: Who is it?

BRINK: It's Mr. Brink. You seem rather tired.

GRANNY: I am kinda tired, Mr. Brink.

BRINK: I thought so. Well, you're to come with me now.

GRANNY [*rousing*]: Come with you? Brink? I don't know any . . . [*Turns and discovers* BRINK *beside her.*] . . . See here, what call have you to come buttin' into a lady's bedroom!

BRINK: I usually come to bedrooms. It's so much more comfortable.

GRANNY: What is?

BRINK: To come with me.

GRANNY: Why should anyone go with you?

BRINK: It's customary.

GRANNY: Oh? Well, you might as well sit down and wait. Because you needn't think I'll stir a step until I've finished this mitten. [*Confidentially.*] I'm narrowin' off at the top now.

BRINK: Yes. I know you are.

GRANNY [*laughs*]: What do you know about knittin'?

BRINK: I don't mean the mitten. I mean you.

GRANNY [*laughs*]: What a fool thing to say. Don't you know a lady from a mitten?

BRINK [*turning away*]: Yes. I know a lady from a mitten.

GRANNY: Now, don't go 'way. You'll just have to wait. I've got to finish this job for my son, Jim. . . . [*Puzzled for a minute, then nods to affirm statement.*] . . . When he drives to Gainesville he says there won't anythin' keep his hands warm but a pair of my mittens. [*Laughs.*] Those boughten things you get at the store—they're no good. A doctor has to be out in all kinds of weather, you know.

BRINK [*smiling*]: He won't need them this year.

GRANNY [*laughs*]: Huh! What do you know about it?

BRINK: Oh, I know many things.

GRANNY: I'll wager I could show you a thing or two about knittin'.

BRINK [*crossing close to bed*]: No doubt. Are you ready now?

GRANNY [*breathlessly*]: Wait . . . just a minute. . . . I'm almost finished. . . . [*Breaks thread.*] . . . There! That's got it! Don't that red stripe look well with the grey?

BRINK: Excellent, my dear. Excellent. Come now. [*He leans over and touches her. She smiles and dies.*]

DIM OUT

CURTAIN

SCENE IV

Exterior: GRAMPS' *backyard, showing porch down left, with cellar and toolhouse attached, up left. Barn is just behind. Apple tree is up right center, with hill behind, town in distance. Right, is picket fence, showing edge of yard, with practical gate, ajar. Silo and other buildings outside of fence. Hill is practical, with walk down to up left center stage. Garden bench center; garden chair left.*

AT RISE: MARTIN'S BOY *is sitting in tree, tugging at his breeches.* DEMETRIA *enters from porch, goes to tree.*

Action is few minutes later than Scene 3.

DEMETRIA [*crossing to center, shouting*]: Come down out of there. I see you.

BOY [*in tree*]: I'm not doing anything. I just . . .

DEMETRIA: You're just a thief, that's what you are.

BOY: I didn't take any apples.

DEMETRIA: You good-for-nothing, you come down from there this minute.

BOY: I can't.

DEMETRIA: You got up all right.

BOY: My pants is caught in behind.

DEMETRIA: Either you come down this minute, or I'll have the law on you.

BOY [*crying*]: I'm not doing anything. I didn't take any apples yet. . . .

DEMETRIA [*crosses to* BOY, *pulls his leg*]: You come down from there. I'll teach you to trespass.

[GRAMPS *and* PUD *enter from between toolhouse and barn.* GRAMPS *carries a stick.*]

GRAMPS [DEMETRIA *turns*]: You'll do what?

DEMETRIA [*defensively*]: There's a boy up that tree.

GRAMPS [*crosses left, below bench*]: And what were you goin' to teach him?

[PUD *follows* GRAMPS *down to below chair left.*]

DEMETRIA [*coming center*]: I should think you'd thank me to catch a trespasser for you.

GRAMPS: And how was you figurin' to teach him not to trespass?

DEMETRIA [*looking at* BOY]: I'd give him a good sound whipping, that's what I'd do.

GRAMPS: You would. [*He raises stick.*] Thanks for tellin' me, Demmie. Because seein' as how there happens to be two trespassers here, I'll just begin with the one that's handiest. . . .
[*He advances on her.*]

DEMETRIA [*stepping right*]: Oh, don't be so silly, Julian.

PUD [*jumping up and down*]: Hit her, Gramps. Hit her on the rump!

DEMETRIA [*crossing to* PUD]: Why . . . you little brat.

GRAMPS [*waving stick*]: You git off my property!

DEMETRIA: All right, Julian Northrup! Maybe you'll find out whose property this is some day!

GRAMPS: You'll find out I can take care of my own.

DEMETRIA: Sometimes the law has something to say about things.
[*She hurries off through gate right.* GRAMPS *stalks her out.* PUD *laughs.* GRAMPS *laughs. Then* BOY *in tree laughs.* GRAMPS *looks up in tree.* BOY *stops laughing suddenly.*]

GRAMPS [*looking in tree*]: Whose boy are you?
[PUD *comes above right of bench.*]

BOY: Jud Martin.

GRAMP: Why're you stealin' my apples?

BOY: I'm hungry.

GRAMPS: Don't your folks give you nothin' to eat?

BOY: Yes, sir.

GRAMPS: So you're apple-hungry?

BOY: Yes, sir.

GRAMPS: Why don't you come down?

BOY: I can't.

GRAMPS: Why can't you?

BOY: My breeches is caught.

GRAMPS: Your breeches is caught.

PUD [*jumping up and down, excitedly*]: Gramps, Gramps! Your wish! He can't come down! He can't come down! He can't come down!

GRAMPS [*hushing* PUD]: Ssh! [*To* BOY] Now, you unloosen your breeches. [BOY *tugs again at his breeches, finds they are loose.*] And come down from there as fast as you can.

BOY [*bewildered*]: Yes, sir. I'm coming. My breeches is loose now.

PUD [*crossing down left*]: Aw, Gramps, you shouldn't have let him unloose his breeches. We could of kept him up there for a million years.

[BOY *comes down from tree,* GRAMPS *collars him.*]

GRAMPS: Now, would that have been nice, son? Now then, I'll teach you to steal. Here. Here. [*He fills* BOY's *pockets with apples.*] The next time you want apples, don't sneak around the back. Walk right up to the front door, ring the bell and ask for some. Will you do that?

BOY: Yes, sir!

PUD: Like hell he will.

[*The boys begin to fight.* BOY *gets* PUD *down on his back.*]

GRAMPS: You fellows stop that! Pud, you lay off that boy. Go along, you.

[GRAMPS *taps* BOY *playfully with stick, chasing him off.*]

BOY: Thanks, Mr. Northrup.

[BOY *goes off right.*]

PUD: Gramps, what'd you stop us for? I had him practical licked.

[PUD *crosses to tree and begins to climb.*]

GRAMPS: Yes, I guess you did. . . . Them apples I gave him'll be pretty bitter, 'cause he didn't steal them.

PUD [*at tree*]: Boost me up, Gramps. Boost me up.

GRAMPS [*crosses to* PUD, *helps him*]: Boost you up! You don't have to steal. Oh, all right. By golly, boy, you're a full-time job. . . . Now, you're up!

PUD [*in tree, shakes finger at* GRAMPS]: Now, you know I can't get down until you let me.

GRAMPS [*laughs, crosses to bench*]: My Lord and Miss Boopydoop, you sure do beat the trolley cars.

PUD: You wished *nobody* could come down until you let them. That was your wish.

GRAMPS [*sits on bench*]: That's right, boy. Guess it was.

PUD: So I can't come down either. I hope you won't keep me up here too long, Gramps.

GRAMPS: Liable to keep you up there all week. Maybe a hundred years. Depends on how I feel.

PUD: Oh, no, Gramps.

GRAMPS: Yep. Might leave you there and go down to Milbaur Park and pick up a few new specimens for our collection.

PUD [*starts to climb large branch*]: Then I'm coming down, Gramps.

GRAMPS: But you can't. You're under my magic spell. Yep, think I'll go along right now . . . good-bye. [*Rises.*]

PUD: Wait a minute, I'm coming with you. [PUD *comes part way down and hangs.*] Gramps, I can't let loose!

GRAMPS: 'Course you can't. You can't let loose till I tell you.

PUD [*frightened*]: But, honest, I can't, Gramps.

GRAMPS [*thundering*]: 'Course you can't. You can't go breaking my spells like that!

PUD [*more frightened*]: Let me down, Gramps! Let me down! Please! My arms is tired! [GRAMPS *laughs.*] Gramps! Gramps! Let me go, let me go! Gramps! Gramps!

GRAMPS: Come on, then. Let go. Let go, honey. [PUD *falls to the ground with a wail.* GRAMPS *hurries to him.*] What's the matter, boy, what's the matter?

PUD [*wailing*]: I couldn't let go!

GRAMPS [*sits beside* PUD]: Of course you could.

PUD: No, I couldn't, Gramps. My hands wouldn't move!

[*He stops crying.*]

GRAMPS: I thought we were just foolin'.

PUD: I was foolin' at first and then my hands wouldn't move. The tree was holdin' me.
[*Looks up at tree.*]

GRAMPS: By golly, you do give a person the creeps sometimes. Dog-gone if I don't believe you really thought that tree was holdin' you.

PUD: It was, Gramps, it was.

GRAMPS: Oh, that old apple tree couldn't hold anybody!

PUD [*turning and pointing at* GRAMPS]: Yes, it could, Gramps. You wished it could.
[MARCIA *enters from porch.*]

MARCIA [*crying*]: Mr. Northrup! Come upstairs! Mrs. Northrup is . . . Mrs. Northrup!
[*She buries her face in her hands.* GRAMPS *and* PUD *continue to look at tree.*]

CURTAIN

SCENE V

Exterior. The tree. A week later. Nearly dusk.
AT RISE: GRAMPS *sits alone on bench. Moody. He is wearing mourning band on arm.* MARCIA *enters from porch.*

MARCIA [*carrying mixing bowl*]: Mr. Northrup.

GRAMPS [*looking up*]: Oh, hello there, Marcy.

MARCIA: Supper's nearly ready. Time you got washed.

GRAMPS: All right, Marcy.

MARCIA [*coming to bench*]: Miss Riffle was just over again.

GRAMPS: Was she?

MARCIA: She's been over every day since the funeral. She keeps asking about your health.

GRAMPS: Damned old hellion. Just waitin' for me to die, ain't she?

MARCIA: Oh, Mr. Northrup. You've got to take care of yourself. If you don't eat any more than you have the last week . . . You've got to keep up your strength, Mr. Northrup.

GRAMPS: All right, Marcy. Thank you.

[*He doesn't move.*]

MARCIA: And Pud seems awfully lonesome lately, too.

GRAMPS: Pud?

MARCIA: He doesn't seem himself at all.

GRAMPS: That so?

MARCIA: When you don't eat, he hardly eats a mouthful either.

GRAMPS: That's what she said. She said "he mimics everything you do."

MARCIA: That's right. He does.

GRAMPS [*suddenly*]: If I'd only got there in time, Marcy!

MARCIA [*sits beside* GRAMPS]: Oh, don't take it so hard, Mr. Northrup.

GRAMPS: We had words and she died before I could take 'em back and say I was sorry.

MARCIA: She understood!

GRAMPS: She died and she didn't forgive me, she died and she didn't forgive me.

MARCIA: She did, Mr. Northrup. She would have for-
given you for anything. . . . Oh, I almost forgot . . .

[MARCIA *runs off quickly, through porch.* PUD *runs
in through gate right. When he see* GRAMPS, *he stops
short, walks slowly around bench.*]

PUD [*right center*]: Gramps!

GRAMPS: Oh, hello there, sonny.

PUD: Shall I sit down here too?

GRAMPS: Sure thing. What makes you think you
shouldn't?

PUD: I think I should.

[*Sits right of* GRAMPS.]

GRAMPS: Gonna have supper in a minute.

PUD: I'm not hungry.

GRAMPS: Gotta eat, boy. Hungry or not hungry.

PUD: Why?

GRAMPS: Keep up your strength. [*He suddenly
clutches* PUD.] There's only me and you left now.
Only me and you. I figure we got to stick together.

PUD: You're damn right.

GRAMPS: Shouldn't cuss, boy.

PUD: Why shouldn't I? *You* say that.

GRAMPS: I shouldn't neither. Your Granny didn't like
it. Let's you and me turn over a new leaf, Pud.

PUD: What for?

GRAMPS: So your Aunt Demmie won't keep on saying
I'm bad for you and won't keep on trying to get you
away from me.

PUD: Aw, we'll kill her.

GRAMPS: By the Lord Harry, I almost wish we could.

PUD [*excited*]: We'll kill her; we'll kill her and we'll put her in the ground. We'll lower the coffing and I'll say . . .

GRAMPS: Hush, boy. Hush!
[*He leans down, puts head in hands.*]

PUD [*touching him*]: What's the matter, Gramps? Are you sick?

GRAMPS: Growin' pains, I guess.
[MARCIA *comes out of house with* GRAMPS' *pipe.*]

MARCIA [*crossing to bench*]: Here's your pipe, Mr. Northrup.

GRAMPS: My pipe, Marcy? Oh, I don't believe I can smoke it, thank you kindly. My throat hurts me a little. Fact is, I don't think I'll ever smoke any more. She didn't like it.

MARCIA: But she did, Mr. Northrup. I know she did.

GRAMPS: Nope. Miss Nellie thought it was a dirty habit. And I guess it is. . . .

MARCIA: She told me I was always to keep your pipe filled.

GRAMPS: Miss Nellie what? When?

MARCIA: Just before she died. I took her up a cup of tea and she caught hold of my hand and said . . . wait, I'll remember her exact words . . . she said: "Marcy . . . Marcy, see that Julian always has his pipe."

GRAMPS: Marcy. . . . You're not just making this up to make me feel good?

MARCIA: No, no, Mr. Northrup. I couldn't do that.

GRAMPS: Give me the pipe.

[*He takes it and tries to light it, but trembles so that* MARCIA *helps him. He smokes.*]

PUD: Does it taste good, Gramps?

GRAMPS: Better'n anything I know, boy.

MARCIA: I'll go finish supper.

[MARCIA *goes off into the house.*]

PUD: Why did your hand wiggle so when you lighted the pipe, Gramps?

GRAMPS: Did it, sonny? Guess I haven't been keepin' up my strength. Do feel kind of shaky. . . .

[BRINK *appears right.*]

BRINK [*crossing to center*]: Good evening.

GRAMPS: Oh, it's you, is it? What do you want?

BRINK: You.

GRAMPS: Can't I ever shut my eyes without you buttin' in?

BRINK: I thought perhaps you'd like to come with me now.

GRAMPS [*takes* PUD *over to his left*]: Now look here, Mr. Brink. I ain't goin' with you at all. I'm goin' to stay right here with this young fellow. And you're about as welcome as a fly on a currant bun, so now you know.

BRINK: Your similitudes are a trifle earthy, but your meaning is clear.

GRAMPS [*turns to* PUD, *laughs*]: My similitudes! What kind of talk is that?

PUD: Sure. What kind of talk is that! He sure talks funny, doesn't he, Gramps?

GRAMPS [*rises, crosses to* BRINK]: Now go on. Get off my property!

BRINK: Now, let's not be difficult about it. Your wife was so charming to me.

GRAMPS: Miss Nellie? Is she well?

BRINK: Sorry. I can't tell you that. Only that she has changed.

GRAMPS: Miss Nellie changed? That's what you think!

BRINK: Oh, my dear man, let's not argue the point, and this time you can't fight me away. [*Pause.*] Come now.

GRAMPS: No, no—I—

BRINK: Come now. Come.

GRAMP: No. No.

[GRAMPS *is stricken with pain. Looks at* PUD.]

BRINK: You're being difficult again. It's so easy and so pleasant. Now don't worry. Look at me.

[BRINK *advances to* GRAMPS, *with hand outstretched. Pause.*]

GRAMPS: Just a minute, please, Mr. Brink. I'd like to have one last apple before I go.

BRINK: Oh, all right.

[GRAMPS *starts to climb the tree, fumbles and gropes at tree.*]

GRAMPS: You wouldn't like to get it for me, would you?

BRINK: Curious request. Oh, why not? [BRINK *climbs tree, points to apples.*] This one? Or this one?

GRAMPS [*backs away to front of bench*]: I don't want none of them! I got you up that tree and you're gonna stay there until I tell you to come down.

[*Wind shakes tree, as* BRINK *struggles to get free. Is bewildered.*]

PUD [*putting arms around* GRAMPS]: You got him, Gramps. You got him!

[GRAMPS *clutches* PUD, *looks at him.*]

GRAMPS: By golly, boy, I believe we have!

CURTAIN

ACT TWO

*The tree. Two hours later. It is dusk. A fence is
being built around the tree.*

At Rise: *Three* WORKMEN *are building fence.* TWO
are stretching barbed-wire. ONE *is settling post at top
of hill, right.* DEMETRIA *enters from house, goes to
gate, looks out, goes to* WORKMEN. BRINK *is invisible.*

DEMETRIA [*to* WORKMAN]: Here you, come here.

WORKMAN [*crossing down to her*]: Yes, ma'am.

DEMETRIA: Has Mr. Northrup told any of you men
why he's building this fence?

WORKMAN: Well, not exactly, ma'am. It's to keep
people away from the tree.

DEMETRIA: Why?

WORKMAN: He says if we touch the tree we are in
danger.

DEMETRIA: Danger of what?

WORKMAN: Well, I'm not sure, ma'am, I thought he
said we were in danger of our lives.

DEMETRIA: That's very interesting. That's what he
said to me too. [*She motions* WORKMAN *away, as*

53

DR. EVANS *and* MR. PILBEAM *enter through gate right.*] Ah, Doctor Evans, Mr. Pilbeam, how do you do? I'm glad you could come. [EVANS *has crossed to porch.*] Julian is just around the corner burying his dog.

EVANS [*going to her down center*]: What does he want us for?

DEMETRIA: He doesn't want you, gentlemen. It was I who asked you to come up. I want you to meet someone.

PILBEAM [*right of* DEMETRIA]: Who?

DEMETRIA: A friend of Julian's—a Mr. Brink.

EVANS: I'm rather busy right now, Miss Riffle.

DEMETRIA: I appreciate that, Doctor, but I thought you would like to meet this friend of Julian's.

EVANS: Well, all right, where is he?

DEMETRIA: Well, just at the moment, he's up in the apple tree.

[*Pause. They look at her surprised, then look up into tree.* DEMETRIA *stands watching them in silence.*]

PILBEAM [*back to her*]: Er—where did you say he was?

DEMETRIA: Right up in that apple tree.

[*They glance up again.*]

EVANS [*crossing up left*]: I don't see anyone up there. [*Crossing down left.*]

DEMETRIA: Oh, no. You can't see him. He's invisible.

PILBEAM: What?

DEMETRIA: He's invisible.—You see, a short while after Julian got Mr. Brink up there, Betty, the old dog, saw him and barked at him. Mr. Brink didn't like that so he became invisible. And right after that, Betty touched her nose to the tree and dropped over dead. Julian and Pud are burying her now.

EVANS: What is this anyway?

PILBEAM: Is this supposed to be a joke, Miss Riffle?

DEMETRIA: What would you say if I told you I believed it was the Gospel truth?

EVANS: 'Fraid I'd say you were crazy.

DEMETRIA: I would be crazy, wouldn't I? And what if I told you that Mr. Brink is a man, just like you, who goes around taking people away with him when it's time for them to die. Now, if I believed that you'd surely say I was crazy, wouldn't you?

EVANS: I'd say you were positively nuts, Miss Riffle.

DEMETRIA: Yes. Well, I don't believe it—but Julian does.

PILBEAM: Come, come, Miss Riffle, what kind of story is this?

DEMETRIA [*sits in chair left*]: An hour ago when I happened to be passing, I saw all these pieces of fence being unloaded from a truck. Naturally, I came back to find out what was going on. Julian told me he was building the fence to keep people away from the tree, because anybody who touched the tree would die.

PILBEAM: Die?

DEMETRIA [*rises*]: And not only that! Touching that tree is the only way anyone can die. There is no more death in the world, Mr. Pilbeam, until Julian lets Mr. Brink come down.

EVANS [*crosses back of* DEMETRIA *to right center*]: See here, Miss Riffle, you don't think Northrup really believes this?

DEMETRIA [*to him*]: Julian is an old man and he's been through a great deal lately. I think it's perfectly obvious what has happened. His mind has just suddenly snapped. Julian Northrup is as crazy as a loon.

EVANS: No, no, I saw Northrup only day before yesterday. He was as sane as any man could be. He's just an old joker. I've known him for years. . . . [*Crosses right.*]

DEMETRIA: You have, Doctor Evans. And Mr. Pilbeam has been his lawyer for years. That's why I've asked both of you to come up. I'm not asking you to take my word for it. I'm simply asking you to see Julian and convince yourselves that what I'm saying is true.

PILBEAM [*with a look to* EVANS]: If Northrup should be insane, you'd have to take Pud, of course, wouldn't you, Miss Riffle?

DEMETRIA: Naturally. I'm next of kin.

EVANS [*crossing upper center right*]: Huh!

PILBEAM: That's what I thought.

DEMETRIA: What do you mean? You don't think I'm making this up about Julian?

PILBEAM: I don't know what to think, Miss Riffle.

DEMETRIA [*two steps to* PILBEAM]: Ever since Nellie Northrup died, Mr. Pilbeam, you've tried to stop my adopting Pud. Even though I told you that was her dying wish.

PILBEAM: I simply said no court of law would believe you, Miss Riffle.

DEMETRIA: I guess a court of law will feel different about it, if they realize a young boy is being brought up by a maniac? [EVANS *puts bag down by gate, crosses down center.*] I'll be frank with you, Mr. Pilbeam, I intend to get that boy away from this insane man's house before something terrible happens. Tonight—if possible! [DEMETRIA *crosses to* EVANS.] There is a way of taking care of such cases immediately, isn't there?

[PILBEAM *crosses up center.*]

EVANS: Well, yes. I'll tell you, I'm not a psychiatrist, Miss Riffle, but if I think Northrup's crazy, I'll talk it over with Grimes. He's the head of the asylum.

DEMETRIA: You will talk it over with him tonight?

EVANS [*crossly*]: When a person's insane you don't usually let him run around loose.

DEMETRIA: Thank you, Doctor Evans, I'll just ask the workmen to . . . [*She crosses up center to* WORKMEN. GRAMPS *is heard bellowing off stage.*] Just a minute, I think he's coming now.

[PILBEAM *crosses right.*]

GRAMPS [*off stage*]: Here you, there. [GRAMPS *enters from top of hill right, followed by* PUD. *They come down the walk.*] What the hell do you mean by gettin' so near to that tree? Didn't I tell you to stay away from that tree on peril of your lives?

PUD [*carries spade*]: What the hell's the idea?

GRAMPS [*still to* WORKMEN]: Now, you fellows, go

on back to that truck and get the rest of that fence unloaded. Get a move on.

PUD [*sits by tree*]: Get a move on.

[WORKMEN *exit up hill*.]

GRAMPS [*crosses to* DEMETRIA *center*]: Now, what in tarnation are you doin' around here again! I told you . . .

DEMETRIA: It's just that I'm so excited about it, Julian.

GRAMPS: And Pilbeam and Evans, eh? By God, you've told them all about it, haven't you? After I told you not to.

DEMETRIA: Why, no, Julian, I haven't told. . . .

EVANS [*crosses to* GRAMPS]: Yes, she's told us all about it. About the tree, the fence, Mr. Brink . . . everything.

GRAMPS [*crosses left*]: I might have known it. I might have known it.

EVANS [*follows* GRAMPS *left*]: Well, what about it, Northrup? What's the answer?

GRAMP: Well, it's the truth, Evans. It's just as true as I'm standin' here.

PILBEAM [*laughing*]: You mean there's somebody sitting up in that tree?

[*He crosses right center*.]

EVANS: And nobody in the world can die any more?

GRAMPS: Nobody can die any more until I say so, unless they touch that tree, or one of them apples, or Mr. Brink himself.

EVANS [*crossing left*]: You're not serious about this, Northrup?

DEMETRIA [*crosses down center*]: Of course he is,

Doctor. He's perfectly serious, aren't you, Julian?

GRAMPS [*crosses center to* DEMETRIA]: Hey there, what the hell are you up to anyway?

DEMETRIA: Why, nothing, Julian. I'm just interested. . . .

GRAMPS: Well, I don't want you to go telling anybody else about Mr. Brink. I got him up there and now I gotta figure out what the hell I'm gonna do with him.

[*Crosses upper center.*]

DEMETRIA: But you don't think you'll be able to keep a thing like this quiet, Julian.

EVANS: Look here, Northrup. Can you talk to Mr. Brink?

GRAMPS: Sure I can talk to him.

EVANS: Have you talked to him since you got him up there?

GRAMPS: Nope. Haven't had time.

EVANS: I wish you'd talk to him now.

GRAMPS: What for? Just so's you can hear him?

EVANS: I just thought, perhaps if you tried to talk to him—well, you'd find out he isn't up there any more.

GRAMPS: Oh, he's up there, all right.

DEMETRIA: Julian, do try to make him talk. I'd love to hear him.

GRAMPS [*crosses to* DEMETRIA]: Oh, you would. [*He turns suddenly and stares at* DEMETRIA. *Slight pause.*] Well, by golly, Demmie, I believe I'll let you. I'll let you all hear him. [DEMETRIA *crosses to* PILBEAM *and* EVANS. GRAMPS *goes to tree.* MARCIA

enters from porch.] Mr. Brink, can you hear me if
I don't shout?

BRINK: Sir?

GRAMPS: See, he calls me "Sir." . . .

DEMETRIA [*to* EVANS *and* PILBEAM]: There, he thinks
someone's answering.

GRAMPS: Well, Mr. Brink, I'm sorry I haven't had
more of a chance to talk to you.

[MARCIA *crosses down left*.]

BRINK: Perhaps I shouldn't say it but I'm not ex-
tremely upset by that.

GRAMPS: You're not mad at me, are you?

BRINK: I think I might justifiably be allowed some
slight irritation.

GRAMPS: Well, I wouldn't have put you there without a damn good reason. I got you up there so this
old hellion couldn't get Pud and the money his father left him.

BRINK: I appreciate that your motive was probably
sincere.

GRAMPS: Now, I got an idea, and it's goin' to settle
once and for all this business of her gettin' Pud.
[*He crosses to* DEMETRIA *and pulls her center*.]
Come here, you. Stand out there. [*To* BRINK.]
You see this old battle-ax here—her name is Demetria Riffle. Have you got anything on your schedule
about when you are supposed to snuff her out?

BRINK: Riffle? There's no such name that has come
to my attention yet.

GRAMPS: Well, Mr. Brink, I'm goin' to keep you up
there until it's time for you to exterminate her.

[GRAMPS *crosses down right*. DEMETRIA *crosses left to* EVANS *and* PILBEAM.]

BRINK: My dear man, that may be a very long time yet. There's no telling how long that woman may hang on.

GRAMPS: Well, that's the way it's goin' to be.

BRINK: But for me to stay here any length of time might be considered by my Superior as a considerable dereliction of duty.

GRAMPS: Can't help it. Them's the terms.

BRINK [*with sigh*]: Ah, well! I was afraid of that. Very well, since you and your tree are so tenacious, I shall have to sit here and wait for Miss Riffle's call.

GRAMPS: Do you think you can hold out that long?

BRINK: My dear man, a human life is like the twinkling of an eye to me.

GRAMPS: Oh, yes, I suppose it is. All right, then, Mr. Brink. [GRAMPS *turns back to others*.] Well, there you are!

[*They all look at him*.]

DEMETRIA: Julian, I'm sorry for you. I really am.

GRAMPS: Sorry for me? You heard what Mr. Brink said, didn't you?

DEMETRIA: No—I—didn't hear this thing in the tree say anything.

GRAMPS: You didn't? [*Turns to* PILBEAM.] You heard Mr. Brink, Pilbeam?

PILBEAM: I'm sorry, Northrup. I didn't.

GRAMPS [*to* EVANS]: Evans!

EVANS [*crosses right center*]: No, Northrup, I didn't. . . .

GRAMPS [*frantically*]: Marcia! [MARCIA *turns away.* GRAMPS *sits in chair left.*] Well, I'll be a . . . what the hell's the matter? Am I goin' nuts?

EVANS [*crosses to* GRAMPS. *Motions* DEMETRIA, PILBEAM *to cross right*]: It's probably just some sort of a dream or something, Northrup. You'll probably get over it in a few weeks and be all right again. [*Crosses right to others.*]

GRAMPS [*softly*]: Didn't no one hear what he said? [*Pause.* EVANS *stands looking at him sadly.*]

PUD [*suddenly*]: He said a human life was like the twinkling of an eye to him.
[*He crosses down to right of* GRAMPS.]

GRAMPS: Ye Gods, that's just what he said! Just what he said! A dream, eh? What else did he say, Pud? [MARCIA *runs into house.*]

PUD: Said he'd have to stay up there 'cause you and the tree was ten . . . ten . . . it was another funny word, Gramps.

GRAMPS: Tenacious!

DEMETRIA [*to* EVANS *and* PILBEAM]: See what he's doing to the boy.

GRAMPS: That's just what he said. [*Rises, crosses right.*] You see where that leaves you.
[*Pause.*]

DEMETRIA: Guess I'm too dull to hear.

GRAMPS: That's it. Must be. Guess you're all too dull to hear.

PILBEAM: Yes, I guess that must be it.

[*They are strangely silent.*]

EVANS [*crosses right center*]: I want to show you something, Northrup.

GRAMPS: Hey, there, what are you goin' to do?

EVANS [*starting to tree*]: I'm going to eat an apple for you.

GRAMPS [*tripping him*]: Hey, you Gol-darned fool, after all I've been tellin' you about them apples. [PUD *hands* GRAMPS *the spade.*] You make one more move toward that tree and I'll brain you.

[DEMETRIA *screams.* EVANS *is on ground.*]

EVANS [*quietly*]: All right, Northrup. Let me up. I won't go near the tree.

GRAMPS: Gol-darn fool, tryin' to commit suicide!

[PUD *sits in chair left.*]

EVANS [*rises*]: All right, Northrup. I just wanted to make sure you weren't joking. [*With look to others.*] Are you going to be home a little later this evening, Northrup?

GRAMPS: 'Course I am.

EVANS: I may be over and—er—talk some more about this.

GRAMPS: All right, Evans.

EVANS: Thanks, well . . .

DEMETRIA: I must go.

PILBEAM: Yes.

[DEMETRIA *and* PILBEAM *ad lib, as they go off.*]

EVANS: Goodbye, Northrup.

GRAMPS: Goodbye, Evans. Sorry I had to be rough with you.

EVANS [*picking up bag*]: That's all right.

GRAMPS: And don't worry about none of your patients dying for a while, yet.

EVANS [*with a look at* GRAMPS]: All right. Goodbye, Northrup.

[*He goes out right.*]

GRAMPS [*crosses left, places spade against house*]: Well, now, back to work, sonny, back to work.

PUD: Why don't they hear Mr. Brink?

GRAMPS: Don't know, boy, guess they're all too busy.

BRINK [*appears*]: Oh, my dear man, that isn't the reason at all.

GRAMPS [*turning to him*]: Oh, hello, Mr. Brink. Why is it only Pud and me can hear you, then?

BRINK: I won't go into it now if you don't mind.

GRAMPS: Just as you say, Mr. Brink. One thing I would like to know though.

BRINK: Well?

GRAMPS: You don't think they'll hold it against Pud what I'm doin' to you?

BRINK: I have neither the inclination nor the authorization to dispense information relevant to your inquiry.

PUD [*laughs*]: He still talks funny.

GRAMPS: Well, guess I'll have to take that chance. Come on, boy. Say goodbye to Mr. Brink.

[*Helps* PUD *up.*]

PUD: 'Bye, Brink.

GRAMPS: Can't you say "Mr. Brink"?

PUD: Goodbye, Mr. Brink—excuse me.

BRINK: That's all right— Goodbye, Pud.

[GRAMPS *and* PUD *start toward hill.*]

GRAMPS: Well, we gotta get that fence finished to-night, boy.

PUD: We gotta work like hell to do it, though, Gramps.

CURTAIN

SCENE II

The living-room. Ten o'clock that night.

AT RISE: GRAMPS *is sleeping in chair right of table, with newspaper over his head.* PUD *is playing with toys on floor, left of* GRAMPS.

PUD [*suddenly*]: The King of Massonia wore his crown upon his seat. [*Pause.*] Hey, Gramps. [*Touches* GRAMPS *on knee.* GRAMPS *pulls paper from his head.*]

GRAMPS: How's that?

PUD: The King of Massonia wore his crown on his seat.

GRAMPS: You don't say. And where did you learn that?

PUD: In Sunday school.

GRAMPS: Don't recall that particular passage myself, sonny. You don't, by any chance, mean the King of Macedonia, do you?

PUD: I guess I mean the King of Massachusetts.

GRAMPS: That's probably it. What did he wear his crown on his seat for?

PUD [*climbing on* GRAMPS' *knee*]: He just wanted to sit on it. [*Noise off stage.*] They're doing a pretty good job on that fence, Gramps.

GRAMPS: Yep, they'll finish it before morning. [PUD *is on* GRAMPS' *knee, showing thumb, bound with adhesive tape.*] What on earth did you do to your thumb?

PUD: I hurt it when I was buildin' the fence. But Marcy put a heap o' tape on it, so I guess it's all right.

GRAMPS [*laughs*]: A heap o' tape. A heap o' tape. Yes, adhesive tape will fix anythin'.

PUD: Gramps, how long before Doctor Evans is coming over?

GRAMPS: Ought to be along any minute now.
[PUD *leans his head back on* GRAMPS' *shoulder and plays with his hair.*]

PUD: Sinkpea, sinkpea, sinkpea.

GRAMPS: How's that?

PUD: Sinkpea.

GRAMPS: What on earth is that?

PUD: Just sinkpea.

GRAMPS: Where'd you hear that word?

PUD: I thought of it myself. I was thinkin' of a boat sinkin', and of a pea, so I said—sinkpea.

GRAMPS: What more natural!

PUD: Say it, Gramps.

GRAMPS: What would I want to go sayin' a fool thing like that for?

PUD: Please, Gramps. Say it!

GRAMPS [*with a look over his shoulder*]: Sinkpea.

PUD: Say it louder.

GRAMPS: Sinkpea! Sinkpea—sinkpea!

[MARCIA *enters from hallway left.*]

MARCIA [*coming left of table*]: What's that, Mr.
Northrup?

GRAMPS: Sinkpea. . . . Oh, hello, Marcy. [*Door-
bell rings off stage.* GRAMPS *puts* PUD *off his lap.*]
There we are. Now, off to bed with you. Here you
are, Marcy. 'Night, boy.
[*Crosses above table to door left. Kisses* PUD *before
he goes.*]

PUD [*wiping his mouth*]: Night, Gramps. I'll see you
early in the morning.
[MARCIA *picks up toys from floor.*]

GRAMPS: Sleep tight. I'll let Dr. Evans in, Marcy.
[*Exits left.*]

PUD [*sleepily*]: Marcy, I bet I sleep like my top tonight.

MARCIA: Of course you will, darling.

PUD: I should have been in bed hours ago.
[*They go off upstairs.*]

GRAMPS [*off stage*]: Come right in, Mr. Grimes. [*He
enters followed by* EVANS *and* GRIMES.] I'm glad to
make your acquaintance.
[EVANS *comes to chair left of table,* GRIMES *above
table right.*]

GRIMES: Yeah.

GRAMPS [*going right*]: Well, set down, Evans. Set
down, Mr. Grimes. Have a nip?

GRIMES: Haven't got time for that, Northrup. We've
got to . . .

EVANS: As a matter of fact, Northrup, I've been telling Mr. Grimes about Mr. Brink and the tree.

GRAMPS [*pulls desk chair around, sits center*]: Now, what did you want to go doin' that for?

EVANS: Well, he's very interested.

GRAMPS [*to* GRIMES]: Don't suppose you believe he's up there?

GRIMES [*chuckling*]: Sure, sure, I believe it. I was just going to ask you to come along with me and talk it over. [*Looks at* EVANS.] Another fellow I'd like to have you meet who wants to hear about it.

GRAMPS: It's this way, Mr. Grimes, I don't want any more people knowin' about this thing until I find out some way of provin' it. This is goin' to be a hard thing to make people believe. 'Tain't everybody that can hear Mr. Brink when he talks. I figger that . . .

GRIMES [*with look to* EVANS]: Oh, what the hell's the use? Now try to get this straight, will you? I'm taking you to the state insane asylum!

[*Pause.* GRAMPS *is dazed.*]

GRAMPS [*softly*]: You're takin' me . . . ? You're takin' me to the insane . . . [*Rises. Looks at* EVANS, *who shifts uncomfortably.*] Demetria!

EVANS [*rises. Below table*]: It's this way, Northrup. . . .

GRAMPS [*softly*]: Demmie! . . . Where is Demmie, Evans?

EVANS: Well, she's . . .

GRAMPS: Where is she?

EVANS: Well, she's outside in the car.

GRAMPS: Waitin', eh? Waitin' for Pud.

EVANS: It's just for observation, Northrup. And she'll just keep Pud until you get back.

GRIMES: Sure. Sure. Now, you come along with me and do as you're told and you may get better soon and can come home again.

GRAMPS [*crosses back to chair right*]: There ain't nothin' wrong with me, Mr. Grimes.

GRIMES: Then we'll find that out.

GRAMPS: Honest, there ain't nothin' wrong with me.

GRIMES: Now, are you coming along like a good fellow or do I have to put a jacket on you?
[*Pause. They watch him.*]

GRAMPS [*softly*]: Sort of looks like I gotta, don't it? [*Moves two steps center, then turns as if to go upstairs.*] Now, I'll just go up and say goodbye to Pud.

GRIMES [*blocking his way*]: No, no, you'll see him tomorrow. They'll bring him up to the asylum.

EVANS: Better come along, Northrup.

GRAMPS: Yes, maybe it's just as well.

GRIMES [*takes hat off table*]: All right. Come on. Let's get goin'.

GRAMPS: Sure. Sure. I'm goin' to go right along with you. Gonna march right up to the bug-house and surprise 'em.

GRIMES [EVANS *crosses to the door left*]: That's the way—surprise 'em.

GRAMPS: I guess it will surprise 'em to see how easy I come along.

GRIMES [*crosses to back of table*]: Sure it will. That's a good idea.

GRAMPS: All right. Come on. [*Starts left with* GRIMES.] Oh, wait!

GRIMES: What's the matter?

GRAMPS: My badge. I've got to have my badge like I wear in parades. I'm a veteran, you know.

GRIMES: Fine! You couldn't march without your badge, now could you?

GRAMPS [*crosses to desk*]: No, siree.

[*As* GRAMPS *rummages in the desk drawer,* GRIMES *winks at* EVANS. EVANS *shakes his head.*]

GRIMES [*crosses to* EVANS]: It's all in knowing how to handle 'em. Sometimes the best way is to humor 'em; but sometimes you got to be tough with 'em.

GRAMPS: Here it is. Afraid for a minute it was upstairs. Now then.

[GRAMPS *turns to* GRIMES *and* EVANS, *holding gun in hand.*]

EVANS [*rushing down left*]: Put that down, Northrup!

GRIMES [*crosses to back of table*]: Yeah, put it down now. Put it down.

GRAMPS [*points finger at them*]: Ah! Ah! You know you got to humor a crazy person. And since you've both made up your minds that I'm crazy you can understand it would drive me wild, if you didn't humor me.

EVANS: Be careful, Northrup. You're going to get yourself into trouble. This is no way of getting out of it.

GRAMPS: Only way that occurs to me at the minute. Now listen, I ain't goin' to no bug-house!

GRIMES: Listen, Northrup . . .

GRAMPS: I ain't goin' to no bug-house and I ain't goin' to let that old she-cat get Pud. But I see I gotta prove that what I been sayin' in reference to a certain Mr. Brink ain't no poppycock.

EVANS: Now be reasonable, Northrup.

GRIMES: Yeah, you can prove it to us later.

GRAMPS: Wait a minute. [*Slight pause.* GRAMPS' *eye lights on* EVANS' *satchel.*] That your medicine kit, Evans?

EVANS: Yes.

GRAMPS: What you got in that kit?

EVANS: Lots of things.

GRAMPS: You got anything in it—poison enough to kill a fly?

EVANS: Of course, but . . .

GRIMES [*advancing*]: You can play with all the flies you want when—

GRAMPS: Play! Do you consider it playin' when a man is willin' to risk his freedom on a fly?

EVANS: What's a fly got to do with it?

GRAMPS: I'll make a bargain with you. And you'd best take it, too, because if you don't I'm just liable to go wild as all hell.

[*He wiggles gun at them.*]

GRIMES: Well, what's the bargain?

GRAMPS: You take the worst poison you got in that bag and put some of it in a tumbler. Then you catch a fly and put him in the poison. If that fly dies, I'll give myself up to you, to the police, to anyone, go to the insane asylum, do anythin' you say. [GRIMES *and* EVANS *look at each other.*] Well?

EVANS: If the fly dies, you'll come along with us without makin' any trouble?

GRAMPS: Yup. I promise. Hope to die. Cross my heart.

EVANS: Well—

GRAMPS [*pointing gun*]: It's the easiest way, Mr. Grimes.

GRIMES [*with look to* EVANS]: All right.

EVANS: O.K.

GRAMPS: You get the poison. I'll get the glasses and [*Pointing with gun.*] Mr. Grimes, you catch a fly. [*Crosses to table up right for tumblers.*]

GRIMES [*crosses down left to* EVANS]: He's crazy, raving crazy.

EVANS: Looks like it. But don't think he won't use that gun! I know the old boy. . . .

GRIMES: O.K. Let him play with the fly. How do we know he'll keep his word, though?

EVANS: I think he will.

GRIMES: The word of a nut—

EVANS [*sharply*]: Well, what do you want to do? Take the gun away from him?

GRIMES [*looking around at gun*]: No, no. Let him do it! No hurry.
[GRAMPS *comes back to table. Puts tumblers down on table center.*]

GRAMPS [*coming around right*]: Of course, look here, a bet ain't a bet that don't cut both ways. If the fly lives, you gotta swear I'm sane.

GRIMES: Well, I don't know.

EVANS: Don't worry. [*Crosses to back of table*.] I know damn well I can kill a fly.

GRAMPS: No, you can't!

EVANS: If I can't kill a fly, I'll quit medicine. [*With look to* GRIMES.] You'll agree to this, won't you, Grimes?

GRIMES: Oh, all right.

GRAMPS: You swear?

EVANS: Yes, we swear, Northrup.

GRIMES: Sure, sure, that's all right. You don't have to worry about us.

GRAMPS: All right. Where's the fly? [GRIMES *advances on* GRAMPS. GRAMPS *puts gun behind his back, facing* GRIMES. GRIMES *stops, backs down left*.] Wait a minute. Here's one.
[*He catches one on window screen*.]

EVANS: Got him?

GRAMPS: Yeah. Now, get the tumbler, get the poison. [EVANS *takes poison and tweezers from his bag*.] Don't get so excited, little fly. You'll be buzzin' around just as good as new pretty soon.
[EVANS *puts tumbler over fly, transfers fly to his hand, then to table*.]

GRIMES: You're the funniest one I've seen, Northrup. [*Laughs*.]

GRAMPS: Yup. Guess I am. [*Laughs*.]

EVANS: All right. [*Pouring poison from bottle to other tumbler*.] Here's enough poison to kill a horse. [*In silence*, EVANS *puts the glasses together*

and drowns the fly, sets the glass down on table.]
And there's your fly!

GRAMPS [*crosses left, looks at fly*]: He ain't much of
a swimmer, is he? [*Crosses right.*] Leave him there.
Let him get his belly full before you take him out.
Well, you been practicin' medicine thirty years,
ain't you, Evans?

EVANS: About that.

GRAMPS: And you still think you can kill a fly, eh?

EVANS [*gently*]: I've always thought I could, Northrup.

GRAMPS: Well, well, you live and learn, Evans, you
live and learn.

[GRAMPS *chuckles.* GRIMES *chuckles.*]

EVANS: All right. He's had time enough.

[*They crowd around as* EVANS *takes out the fly
with tweezers. He puts him on newspaper and they
peer at him.*]

GRAMPS [*crosses to chair right of table, sits*]: Looks
kinda sick, don't he?

GRIMES: If I ever saw anything deader I don't know
what it is.

EVANS: He's dead, Northrup.

[GRAMPS *stirs the fly. Pause. They watch it.*]

GRIMES: Don't tell us we don't know when something's dead.

GRAMPS: Wait a minute. Give this fly a chance. You
can't come to yourself all of a sudden.

GRIMES: You're tough all right, Northrup. Tough
but crazy. [*Pause. To* EVANS.] Well?

EVANS: He'll come along, I think.

GRIMES: Let's get going then.

[*They look at* GRAMPS. *He seems bewildered and beaten but he stares at the fly.*]

EVANS [*crosses to* GRAMPS]: All right, Northrup. A bet's a bet.

GRAMPS: Well, I'll be God-damned. . . .

[*Touches fly with gun.*]

EVANS: Come on now. Put down that gun.

[GRAMPS *suddenly looks up, excited.*]

GRAMPS: Wait a minute . . . wait a minute—he moved. . . .

[*Others look at the paper, quickly.*]

EVANS: Huh?

GRAMPS [*rises*]: Look, look! He's drunk as a lord but we didn't say anythin' about that. He's movin' right across that God-damned piece of paper!

[GRAMPS *follows fly around the room.*]

EVANS: I'll be damned! I'll be—

GRIMES: Jesus Christ!

EVANS: What is this, Northrup?

GRIMES: You didn't give him enough poison, Evans.

EVANS: I gave him enough poison to kill a million flies.

GRIMES: Something went wrong.

EVANS: You saw the fly in the poison yourself.

GRAMPS: Well, now will you believe what I've been tellin' you about Mr. Brink?

[*Pause.* GRIMES *turns to him, pulling out handcuffs.*]

GRIMES [*crosses to front of table*]: To hell with that! Put down that gun, Northrup.

GRAMPS [*crosses to center*]: Hey, wait a minute, you said—

GRIMES: Put it down now! I don't know what kind of a trick this is—

EVANS: You promised him, Grimes.

GRIMES: I came to get him and, by God, I'm going to do it! What's a promise to a lunatic?

GRAMPS: So you don't believe it yet, eh? Even after I proved it to you?

GRIMES [*softly*]: You crazy bastard—

EVANS: Look out, Grimes. Wait a minute!

[EVANS *pushes* GRIMES *back left.*]

GRAMPS: And you ain't goin' to keep your word, eh? Well, by God, there's another way of provin' it and it looks like I got to use that way right now.

EVANS [*crosses up center*]: For God's sake, Northrup! What—

GRAMPS: I'm goin' to make another experiment and I want you to witness it.

GRIMES [*going toward* EVANS]: He's crazy as hell! He's dangerous!

EVANS: What are you going to do, Northrup!

GRAMPS: Evans, at this close range if a man was shot right through the belly, he'd die, wouldn't he?

EVANS: Good God, man!

GRIMES: Look out there, Northrup!

GRAMPS: Wouldn't he?

EVANS: Yes, of course, but—

GRAMPS: That's all I want to know.

[*He fires.* GRIMES *crumples up.* EVANS *rushes to him.*]

GRAMPS: Now, don't worry. He ain't goin' to die.

[EVANS *has been bending over* GRIMES. *He straightens up and looks at* GRAMPS.]

EVANS: You crazy fool! He'll be dead in an hour.

GRAMPS [*at window*]: Stay up there, Mr. Brink. If you come down now, by God, I'm in a hell of a fix.

CURTAIN

SCENE III

The tree. Dawn.

AT RISE: EVANS *is holding long fishpole through fence. He pulls it out; there is long, gray object on end of it. He kneels beside it, studies it carefully with magnifying glass.* MARCIA *comes out from porch, opens shutters on living-room window. Sees* EVANS.

MARCIA [*startled*]: Oh. [EVANS *looks up with a start.*] Oh, good morning, Dr. Evans. I didn't know you were here.

EVANS: Good morning, Marcia.

MARCIA: Did you want to see Mr. Northrup?

EVANS: Why—why, yes, I did. Is he up yet?

MARCIA: Yes. He and Pud are just finishing breakfast. I'll tell him you're here. He'll be right out.

EVANS: Yes, yes, do that.

MARCIA: Is anything the matter?

EVANS: No—I've been up all night.

MARCIA [*pointing*]: Is that a mouse, Dr. Evans?

EVANS: Yes, Marcia, that's a mouse.

MARCIA: Oh.

[*She looks at him wonderingly and goes in. Pause.*
EVANS *examines mouse again; gets up, puts pole back
through fence; stands looking at tree.*]

EVANS: Hello. [*Pause. No answer.*] Hello up there.
[*Pause. No answer.* PILBEAM *enters from gate
right, stands looking at him.*] Hello.

PILBEAM: Hello.

[EVANS *turns sharply.*]

EVANS [*crosses center*]: Oh, hello, Pilbeam. I was
just—er—

PILBEAM [*crosses center*]: Feeling all right?

EVANS: Of course. Why?

PILBEAM: I just wondered—well, what do you want to
see me about?

EVANS: Thought I might need you.

PILBEAM: Oh. [*Pause.* PILBEAM *watches* EVANS *curi-
ously.*] Hear you didn't lock Northrup up last
night.

EVANS: That's right.

PILBEAM: How's that?

EVANS: He isn't crazy.

PILBEAM: What?

EVANS [*louder*]: He's not crazy.

[*Crosses up left, picks up fishpole.*]

PILBEAM: Oh. [*Pause.*] What you got there?

EVANS: Fishpole.

PILBEAM: Going fishing?

EVANS: Been fishing.

PILBEAN: Catch much? [*Goes left, looks at fishpole, sees mouse.*] Well, that's a mouse.

EVANS [*crosses down left*]: Yeah. That's a mouse.

PILBEAM [*crosses down center*]: Well, what the hell's the matter with you, Evans?

EVANS: What do you mean—what's the matter?

PILBEAM: You got me out of bed.

EVANS [*crosses center*]: Wait a minute, Pilbeam. Now, don't get excited. We got to keep our heads. Because something's happened that'll turn this world upside-down, unless we can stop it. And you gotta help me.

PILBEAM: Uh?

EVANS: Northrup shot Grimes last night, Pilbeam.

PILBEAM: Good God!

EVANS: Shot him right through the belly. He had internal hemorrhages and it was an hour before I could get him to the hospital.

PILBEAM: What did he shoot him for?

EVANS [*looks at tree*]: He was experimenting.

PILBEAM: He was—experimenting!

EVANS: Wait a minute, Grimes is all right.

PILBEAM: All right?

EVANS: He's practically well. That's the trouble. According to everything I know about medicine, Grimes should have died last night, Pilbeam. But he didn't. [*Wipes face, crosses to bench center and sits.*] Plenty of things should have died last night. But they didn't. [*He pauses for a second; continues in a confused voice.*] I've been up all night, trying to kill something. [*He rises, crosses to* PILBEAM.]

I've experimented on everything I could get my hands on. Insects. Bugs. I've tried to kill every stray cat or dog I could find. I couldn't kill a damned thing. Except that mouse. [PILBEAM *silent*.] And do you know how I killed him? I tied him to the end of this fishpole and touched him to that tree.

PILBEAM: Look here, Evans, you've been up all night—

EVANS: Oh, for Christ . . . [*Crosses to center, by gates of fence*.] Don't see anything up there, do you?

[PILBEAM *has followed him to left of center*.]

PILBEAM: Of course not.

EVANS [*crosses to left center*]: Hear anything?

PILBEAM: Not a rustle.

EVANS: Neither do I. But if there is anything up there, by God, it's got to come down. It's got to come down. And you got to help me!

[*They both look back at tree*. GRAMPS *enters, slams screen door. They whirl, startled*.]

GRAMPS: Howdy, Evans. Howdy, Pilbeam.

PILBEAM: Oh, hello, Northrup.

EVANS [*crosses to center*]: Hello.

GRAMPS [*crosses down left*]: How's Mr. Grimes doin'?

EVANS: Seems to be doing all right.

GRAMPS [*chuckles*]: Glad to hear it. Nasty accident. [*Sits in chair left*.] Well, set down. What can I do for you?

[*Pause*. EVANS *crosses to bench, sits*. PILBEAM *crosses to right of center*.]

EVANS: Guess I owe you an apology, Northrup.

GRAMPS: No, you don't. Wouldn't have any respect for you if you believed a thing like this at first. You're a doctor. . . . [*To* PILBEAM.] Kinda interestin', ain't it, Pilbeam?

PILBEAM: Why—er—of course—very interesting.

GRAMPS: Awful nice sort of chap, Mr. Brink is. Real friendly.

BRINK: Thank you very much.

GRAMPS [*rises*]: Oh, mornin', Mr. Brink. Didn't know you were up yet.

[EVANS *rises, looks at* GRAMPS, *the tree, then sits.* PILBEAM *looks at* GRAMPS, *then the tree.*]

BRINK: Oh, yes. I've had a lovely morning. I've had a mouse in my face.

GRAMPS [*looks at* EVANS]: What! Gol-darn it, what you been up to, Evans? Have you been shovin' a mouse in my friend Brink's face?

PILBEAM [*crosses to center*]: Good God, how do you know that?

GRAMPS: Mr. Brink told me, just now.

PILBEAM: Good God, I've got to go!

[*He starts rapidly out right.*]

EVANS [*rises, crosses to* PILBEAM]: Wait a minute, Pilbeam.

[PILBEAM *hesitates.*]

PILBEAM: I've got a busy day, Jim. I got a lot of work to do—

EVANS [*takes* PILBEAM *by arm, crosses to center,* PILBEAM *crosses down right*]: Stick around, Pilbeam.

GRAMPS [*crosses to bench, sits*]: Sure, stick around.

This is a sort of special occasion. In fact, this is the mornin' Demmie figured I'd be in the nut-house. Yes, sir, I'm feelin' right good this mornin'. Pud's feelin' pretty spry. Mr. Brink sounded pretty pert. Everybody's feelin' fine—'cept Demmie. God bless her!

EVANS: Northrup?

GRAMPS: Yeah.

EVANS [*crosses to right of bench*]: There's a man in my hospital who's been suffering for ten years. He's in constant pain.

GRAMPS: I'm real sorry, Evans.

EVANS: Day before yesterday, I decided to operate on him. The operation wasn't successful. He's in more pain now than he ever was.

GRAMPS: Well, Evans, I'm real sorry to hear that.

EVANS: I expected him to die last night. I hoped he would.

GRAMPS: Yeah.

EVANS: There's a nice old lady up in 2C, Mrs. Trenner, remember her?

GRAMPS: The old lady who used to have all the dogs?

EVANS: Yeah.

GRAMPS: By God, I'd forgot all about her.

EVANS: Everybody has. She's been in there for six years, in bed. She hasn't got much left. Only one idea—to die. And this is what's happening in just one small hospital, you know. In a small town. There are two in Gainesville. There are several million in the world, aren't there—full of people just like that.

GRAMPS: I'm sorry for all those people—sorry for all of 'em—but if you're hintin' for me to let Mr. Brink down, you're off on the wrong track.

[EVANS *looks at* GRAMPS *for a moment.*]

EVANS: What do you think is going to happen, Northrup, in the next few days when people find out there's no more death?

PILBEAM: But it isn't true—

EVANS [*crosses to* PILBEAM]: No more death. Think about it for a minute. Nobody died last night. Nobody's going to die tonight. Or tomorrow night. Nobody's going to die . . . [*Looks at* GRAMPS.] . . . until Northrup says they can. What do you think about that?

PILBEAM: It's absurd.

EVANS: That's right. It's absurd. [*Facing* GRAMPS.] Five years from today this world will be so overcrowded that it won't be fit to live in . . . think of the disease . . .

GRAMPS: I don't give a damn! I don't care what happens! I've got Mr. Brink up there and he's gonna stay there!

EVANS [*crosses to bench*]: He can't, Northrup. You gotta let him down.

GRAMPS: Why should I? I'm lookin' after Pud and myself.

EVANS: Who the hell are you?

GRAMPS: I'm the feller that got Mr. Brink up that tree and up that tree he's gonna stay until I'm good and ready to let him down.

[*Rises, crosses left and faces house.*]

PILBEAM [*frightened*]: Well, I've got to get back to the office. I've got work to do. I've got a hell of a lot of work to do today. 'Bye, Northrup. [*No answer.*] Goodbye, Evans. [*No answer. He looks at tree.*] Goodb—

[*Goes out right.*]

GRAMPS [*crosses to bench, sits*]: Look here, Evans, 'tain't that I'm afraid to go. I ain't afraid of dyin'. Might be real pleasant to see what's comin' next. But, you see, there's Pud. I just want to stick around in case he needs me.

[*Pause.*]

EVANS: Have you ever seen a man a hundred and ten years old, Northrup?

GRAMPS: Yep. I seen one pretty near that old once. Old Fred Brown's father. Poor old devil— Hey, what the hell are you drivin' at?

EVANS: I was just thinking—by the time Pud's a young man, you'll be getting about that age yourself.

GRAMPS: No. No. When I saw myself gettin' like that old guy was I'd let Mr. Brink come down and take me.

EVANS: Oh, no, you wouldn't.

GRAMPS: Yes, I would.

EVANS: You wouldn't be able to see yourself getting like that. You'd be too far gone by that time. You might even forget Mr. Brink was up there. [*Pause.* GRAMPS *sits, thinking.*] You gotta let him down, Northrup.

[*Pause.*]

GRAMPS [*softly*]: I don't want to be no nuisance to Pud—

EVANS: You've got to let Mr. Brink come down to-day. I warn you—I'll do everything I can to make you. Better think it over. [*Crosses to tree, picks up bag*.] I'll be back in an hour. [*Starts out, then hesitates*.] Well, thanks for not letting me eat that apple yesterday.

GRAMPS: You kin have one now, if you want it.

EVANS: No, thanks. Well—goodbye, Northrup.

GRAMPS: Goodbye.

EVANS: I'm—I'm sorry.

GRAMPS: Yeah. [EVANS *goes out, leaving* GRAMPS *sitting and thinking*.] Mr. Brink, if I let you come down, you're bound and determined you're gonna take me, ain't you?

BRINK: You will be the first.

GRAMPS: That's what I thought. . . . No way of getting out of that, is there?

BRINK: None.

GRAMPS: No, I didn't think so.

BRINK: It would seem to me that you had got out of a great deal already.

GRAMPS: I just wondered. I just wondered. Don't get upset. . . . [*Rises and crosses to tree*.] . . . Mr. Brink, do you think Evans is right about me and Pud? Think maybe I might become a nuisance to the boy?

BRINK: My dear man, there's no doubt about it.

GRAMPS [*turns and faces upstage*]: Hmmn.

[PUD *comes out of the house acting like an engine.*]
PUD [*in the house*]: Here comes Casey down the track
. . . bingety, bingety, bing. . . . [*Enters.*] . . .
Here comes Casey down the track . . . bingety,
bingety, bing . . . [*Down around chair left.*] . . .
choo, choo, choo . . . [*Across stage to down stage
right.*] . . . choo, choo, choo. . . . [*Stops.*] Say,
God, you are standing there in the middle of my
track. Get out of the way, God; get off my rail-
road track or I'll run over you. . . . I guess I'll
have to strike you dead, Casey. . . . BOOM! . . .
Now, look what you did, God, you wrecked my
train all to splinters. Now I have to get a new engine. . . . All right, Casey, here's a new engine.
. . . [GRAMPS *walks slowly down to left of bench,
watching* PUD.] . . . Thanks, God. Get on and I'll
give you a ride. Here we go . . . choo, choo, choo
. . . ding, ding. . . . Get out of the way, everybody. Get out of the way. Here comes God and
Casey Jones. . . . Toot, toot! [*He stops and sees*
GRAMPS. *Continues till he bumps into him.*] Toot,
toot, choo, choo. . . . [*Hugs* GRAMPS.] I love you,
Gramps, I love you more'n my engine!

CURTAIN

SCENE IV

The tree. Toward close of same day.
AT RISE: GRAMPS *stands behind bench center, with*

PUD *to his right.* SHERIFF BURLINGHAME, DEMETRIA *and* EVANS *are moving across stage, from left to right.* MARCIA *is just coming out on porch, stands left.*

GRAMPS: Just read the last part of that document again, Sheriff. Where Dr. Evans signed. . . .

SHERIFF [*down right*]: All right, Northrup. "Dr. James Evans, having testified that the said Julian Northrup is incapable of managing himself and his property, it is the order of this Court that he be committed to the Gainesville Institution for the Insane, according to the Laws of this State and it is further ordered that the custody of the child, John Gilford Northrup, be awarded to his aunt, Demetria Riffle."

GRAMPS: Thank you, Sheriff. [*Turns to* EVANS.] You've kinda fixed me up good and proper, ain't you?

EVANS: I warned you I'd do anything I could.

GRAMPS [*to* SHERIFF]: So, Evans has told you I'm crazy, ain't he?

SHERIFF: I guess there's no doubt about that, Northrup.

DEMETRIA [*crosses to center*]: I'll be good to the boy while you're in the asylum, Julian. I really will. . . . Come, Pud, you're to come home with me now.

PUD [*clutching* GRAMPS]: Gramps!

SHERIFF [*moving up right*]: Come along, Northrup.

GRAMPS: Wait a minute. [*They all stop.*] I'd like to speak to Pud a minute first.

[EVANS *and* SHERIFF *look at each other.*]

EVANS [*motions* SHERIFF *and* DEMETRIA *to go out*]: You two, wait outside a moment. [*Crosses right center.*] I'm sorry, Northrup, but I've given you all day to make up your mind. I can't wait any longer. So you're going to the insane asylum.

GRAMPS: You're pretty smart, ain't you, Evans? You figger I won't go to the nut-house. You figger I'll let Mr. Brink down instead.

EVANS: I'm hoping you will.

GRAMPS: You figger long as I lost the boy, I don't much care what happens to me.

EVANS: That's what I figure, Northrup.

GRAMPS: All right. You're a pretty smart feller. [*He motions* EVANS *away.* EVANS *joins the others.*]

PUD: What's the matter with Dr. Evans, Gramps?

GRAMPS: Guess he's kinda sorry, boy. [*Crosses to front of bench, sits right.*]

PUD: What's he sorry for?

GRAMPS [MARCIA *crosses upstage*]: Come here a minute.

PUD [*sits left of* GRAMPS]: O.K.

GRAMPS [*looks at* PUD, *turns away to get up his courage*]: I'm goin' away, boy.

PUD: Where, Gramps?

GRAMPS: Where the woodbine twineth.

PUD: You goin' with Mr. Brink?

GRAMPS: Yep, I'm goin' with Mr. Brink. You see, your Gramps is gettin' to be a pretty old man. And when you get to be a pretty old man you begin to get kinda tired.

PUD: Are you tired?

GRAMPS: Right at this minute, I'm pretty dog-gone tired.

PUD: Let's lie down and rest.

GRAMPS: That's just what I'm gonna do. But the only way an old man can really lie down and rest is to go with Mr. Brink.

PUD: I'll go with you, Gramps.

GRAMPS: No, you can't go with me, boy. You've got your whole life ahead of you.

PUD: Don't want my whole life ahead of me. I want to go with you. I love you, Gramps. [*Puts arms around* GRAMPS.]

GRAMPS: Shouldn't love me that much, boy. You see, Pud, I been thinkin' things over. Maybe it ain't such a good thing for you to be livin' with me any more. And, you know, maybe your Aunt Demetria ain't as much of a pismire as we thought she was. [PUD *rises and backs down center.*]

PUD: Gramps!

GRAMPS: No, sir, maybe she ain't. Maybe it'd be better if you was to go over to your Aunt Demetria's house and live with her. [PUD *backs further away.*] What's the matter, boy?

PUD: Don't you love me any more, Gramps?

GRAMPS: Pshaw, boy, I'm just tryin' to make you understand—

PUD: Gramps, you don't love me any more.

GRAMPS: Of course I do. It's just that I gotta go away.

PUD [*crosses to bench, sits*]: But I'll go with you, Gramps.

GRAMPS: But you can't, boy, you can't.

PUD: Please, Gramps, please!

GRAMPS: No.

PUD: Then I don't love you any more either. . . . I don't love you any more either. . . .

[*He turns and runs into house, crying.*]

GRAMPS: Wait a minute, boy, wait a minute.

BRINK: That's the better way.

GRAMPS: Maybe so.

BRINK: He will forget.

GRAMPS: Maybe so.

[SHERIFF, DEMETRIA *and* EVANS *come back.*]

SHERIFF: What about it, Northrup?

GRAMPS: Oh, I ain't goin' with you. I'm goin' with Mr. Brink. Didn't Evans tell you about Mr. Brink?

SHERIFF: Oh, yeah. He did. Well, get it over with. We haven't got all night.

EVANS: Take it easy, Sheriff. . . . Northrup, would you rather we left you alone?

GRAMPS: No. As a matter of fact, I'd like to have somebody around.

[EVANS *turns upstage.* DEMETRIA *crosses to* GRAMPS. SHERIFF *reads document.*]

DEMETRIA [*going to him*]: Well, Julian . . .

GRAMPS: Demmie, honest to God, will you be good to Pud?

DEMETRIA: I'll be good to him, Julian.

GRAMPS: Will you see he gets some fun out of life?

DEMETRIA: I will.

GRAMPS: Will you not keep huggin' him all the time like you do?

DEMETRIA: I'll be good to Pud, Julian. You don't have to worry. I have wonderful plans for him already.

GRAMPS: What plans you got for him?

DEMETRIA: Well, I'm going to start right in getting him ready to go to school next year.

GRAMPS: How d'ye mean, gettin' him ready?

DEMETRIA: I'm gonna start teaching him things myself, Julian. So that when he gets to school, he'll be way ahead of any of the others.

GRAMPS: Ain't you gonna let him play any?

DEMETRIA: Of course, Julian. He'll have his play period. But now he'll have education too. I'll begin to form his mind. . . .

GRAMPS: His mind's formin' all right as it is.

DEMETRIA: And I'll teach him little poems to recite.

GRAMPS: Oh, my God!

DEMETRIA: I'll teach him how to behave nicely, Julian. How to say "Yes, sir" and "No, sir" and how to curtsey when older people—

GRAMPS: Curtsey! Pud!

DEMETRIA: And by the time Miss Ramsdell's school opens in the Fall . . .

GRAMPS: Miss Ramsdell's school is a girls' school!

DEMETRIA: Not any more, Julian. They're going to have three little boys in it next year.

GRAMPS: You're gonna make Pud into a sissy! By God, you are still a pismire! I'm gonna change my mind. I ain't goin' with Mr. Brink. I'm gonna stay right here and take care of Pud.

EVANS [*sharply*]: Northrup! How can you take care of Pud if you're in the asylum?

GRAMPS: Oh.

EVANS: Because that's where you'll be.

GRAMPS: Yeah. Well, what the hell am I gonna do? [*Slight pause.*] Well, no use stretchin' it out. 'Bye, Marcy.

MARCIA: Oh, Mr. Northrup.

EVANS [*crossing to* GRAMPS]: I realize what I'm asking you to do, Northrup. [*Crosses left.*]

GRAMPS: Yeah. . . . Well, Mr. Brink, looks kinda like the time has come.

[GRAMPS *crosses to gates.*]

BRINK: Yes, the time has come now.

GRAMPS: I expect you're all ready.

BRINK: All ready as soon as you say the word.

GRAMPS: Well, I'll just open the gates, then, so's you don't have to climb this here fence.

BRINK: That will be more convenient. I've had quite enough climbing for a while. [MARCIA *down left to chair.* GRAMPS *opens gates.*] I hope you ain't goin' to hold nothin' against me, Mr. Brink.

BRINK: We'll see. We'll see.

GRAMPS: Remember the only reason I got you up there was to keep Demmie from gettin' the boy.

BRINK: I've taken that into consideration.

GRAMPS: I wasn't cheatin'. I was gonna let you down as soon as you had word you was to take her.

BRINK: I know. I know.

[DEMETRIA *laughs.*]

GRAMPS [*looking at* DEMETRIA]: Don't suppose by any chance you've had any word about takin' her yet.

BRINK: No, there's been no call for Miss Riffle. There probably won't be for years.

GRAMPS [*suddenly*]: What's that? You say you were supposed to take her an hour ago?

BRINK: No, no. I said I probably wouldn't take her for years.

GRAMPS: My God, why didn't you tell me, Mr. Brink? Why, if you're supposed to take Demmie too—

BRINK: But I am *not* supposed to take her!

EVANS [*crosses to end of bench left*]: Northrup, did he really say that?

GRAMPS: Yep. Says he was supposed to take Demmie an hour ago. This changes everything. Come on, Demmie!

[*He drags* DEMETRIA *to tree.*]

DEMETRIA [*breaking away from him*]: No— No, Julian. This is absurd! This is—! Dr. Evans.

EVANS: I'm sorry, Miss Riffle. But when a person's time comes . . .

DEMETRIA: But—there isn't really anyone up in that tree— This is all so—so silly.

GRAMPS: Thank you, Mr. Brink, for takin' Demmie. I wonder if you'd do one more thing. I wonder if after you've taken Demmie, you'd just slip the Sheriff in for good measure.

SHERIFF: Hey—what th' hell—

GRAMPS: The old stiff's tryin' to take me to the nuthouse—

EVANS [*crosses to* GRAMPS]: Good God, Northrup! Do you know what you're doing? This is practically murder!

DEMETRIA: M-m-murder! D-d-doctor! M-m-murder!

EVANS: Listen you, all of you, Northrup's as sane as
any one here.

SHERIFF: What's that? Hey, what is this, anyway?

EVANS: Northrup's not insane. You realize what he's
going to do? Death is up in that tree. Northrup's
talking to him. If he lets him down you're as good
as dead, both of you.

DEMETRIA: What! What? I don't believe it—

BRINK: This is—

GRAMPS: Ssh! Ssh!

BRINK: This is the wildest absurdity I ever heard. You
know perfectly well I have no authorization to take
any of these people. It is utterly out of the question.

GRAMPS: What's that? You say you'll take the Sheriff
too? Thank you, Mr. Brink. I appreciate that a
great deal.

DEMETRIA [*crosses left center. Hysterically*]: I don't
believe it—! You can't frighten me! I didn't hear
anything up in that tree! I didn't hear a blessed
thing!

MARCIA [*crosses right to* GRAMPS. *Suddenly*]: I did!
I heard him!

GRAMPS [*crosses down center*]: Eh? What's that?

MARCIA: I heard him! I heard Mr. Brink!

GRAMPS: You did— Now look here, Marcy!

DEMETRIA: You d-didn't—

MARCIA: I did! I did! I heard him just as plain as I
hear you.

[DEMETRIA *looks at* EVANS.]

GRAMPS: But, Marcy—

MARCIA [*quiets him with gesture*]: And he said that if he could just come down he would take anyone Mr. Northrup asked him to.

[GRAMPS *turns right, hiding laughter with his hand.*]

DEMETRIA: He didn't! He didn't say he was going to take me?

MARCIA: Oh, yes, he did, Miss Riffle. He said he was going to take you—first!

[DEMETRIA *sits on bench.*]

BRINK: That girl—

GRAMPS: Ssh! Ssh!

BRINK: That girl cannot hear a word I say. She is the most inordinate liar I ever met.

GRAMPS: Hear him then, Marcy?

MARCIA: Yes.

GRAMPS: What did he say? Now, be careful.

MARCIA: He said to please hurry and let him down. He's getting nervous and can't stand it another minute.

[*Crosses left.*]

GRAMPS: Yup. That's just what he said. So I better get started. Don't want to make him any angrier.

BRINK: That would be impossible. You let me down!

GRAMPS: Well, goodbye, everybody. But then I'll be seein' you two in a second. Now I'm gonna start the magic words. [*Takes* DEMETRIA *and* SHERIFF *by hand.*] Come on, Demmie. Sheriff. Line up. Here we go. Off to glory!

[*He starts mumbling.* SHERIFF, DEMETRIA *and* GRAMPS *walk around in circle.*]

BRINK: Stop that monkey-business and let me down.

EVANS: Stop it, Northrup!

DEMETRIA: Stop him! Stop him, somebody! Stop him.

SHERIFF: Hold on there, Northrup. Hold on!

EVANS [*grabbing* GRAMPS]: Stop it, Northrup! Stop it! We'll do anything you want us to.

SHERIFF [*tears up adoption paper*]: Look, Northrup, look.

GRAMPS: All right! . . . Now, you keep your hands off my boy, Demmie.

DEMETRIA [*crosses upper right*]: I will, Julian, I will.

GRAMPS: And you keep the hell away from me, too.

DEMETRIA: I will, Julian. I'll keep the hell away from you, too.

GRAMPS [*turns to tree*]: All right. Mr. Brink, from now on, anybody who tries to make me let you down you gotta take them too.

BRINK: I will not! I will not!

GRAMPS: Thank you very much. . . . Now, you get out of here. All of you. I'm gonna stay right here and take care of Pud. I don't care if the whole damn world goes to hell. Git out of here. Git off my property. Go on. Go on! If you ask me you got off pretty lucky. [*They all go off right.* MARCIA *crosses to bench, crying, sits.*] Marcy, I love yuh. [*Crosses to bench, sits.*] By God, I love yuh. And there ain't nothin' in this world can stop us now. Just you and me and Pud. Nothin' in the world can stop us, now.

BRINK [*appears*]: Which world do you mean?

GRAMPS: What's that, Mr. Brink?

BRINK: Which world do you mean?

GRAMPS: Why—I don't understand, Mr. Brink.

BRINK: Of course you don't. My poor man!

MARCIA: What did he say, Mr. Northrup?

GRAMPS: He said: "My poor man." And I didn't like the way he said it, Marcy. I didn't like the way he said it.

CURTAIN

SCENE V

The tree. Few minutes later. It is dark.

AT RISE: GRAMPS *and* MARCIA *enter from house, looking for* PUD.

GRAMPS: Pud! Pud!

MARCIA: Where are you, Pud?

GRAMPS: We got to find him, Marcy. We got to find him. I got to explain to him.—Hey, boy, where are you?

MARCIA: Pud!

GRAMPS: You didn't see nothin' of him at all?

MARCIA: Not a thing. Maybe he went over to see Jimmy.

GRAMPS: You run over and see, Marcy. Don't think he'd stay over there this late. You go on.

MARCIA: I'll be right back, Mr. Northrup.
[*Exits right.*]

GRAMPS: Pud! Hey, Pud! Where are you, boy?

Time to come home now. Hey, boy, where are you? Pud! Pud!

[GRAMPS *goes off right, calling for* PUD. PUD *comes out of cellar up left. He is sniffling. He walks down to chair left center.* MR. BRINK *appears.* PUD *carries some belongings in a handkerchief.*]

BRINK: Pud!

PUD [*tearfully*]: Hello there, Mr. Brink.

BRINK: What's the matter, Pud?

PUD: My Gramps doesn't love me any more.

BRINK: He doesn't?

PUD: No. Didn't you follow the conversation?

BRINK: Yes, what are you going to do, Pud?

PUD: I'm going to run away. Then he'll be sorry.

BRINK: What have you got there?

PUD [*showing them*]: These are some cookies I got. . . . And this is my watch fob Gramps wrote on for me. . . . And a couple of specimens.

BRINK: And you're really going to run away?

PUD: 'Course I am.

BRINK: I wouldn't if I were you.

PUD: You would too.

BRINK: They'll only find you and bring you back. You're not big enough to run away, my little man.

PUD: I am so! And I'm not your little man! I'm not a little man at all. I'll spit in your eye.

BRINK: You might find that difficult.

PUD: Why?

BRINK: I'm afraid you couldn't reach me.

PUD: I could too.

BRINK: You would be afraid.

PUD: I'm not afraid of the biggest giant on earth.

BRINK: How do you know I'm not the biggest giant on earth?

PUD: Because you're in the littlest tree.

BRINK: There is a certain logic in that. Your mind is taking shape. That's too bad that has to happen.

PUD: Why?

BRINK: Because man's logic is the most pitiful thing about him. It stands in his way. It confuses him, so that he can't quite see the giants. You won't be able to see them much longer.

PUD: Aw, I will too.

BRINK: No, you will not. Not until you are as old as your grandfather. Then you will be able to see them again.

PUD: Nuts.

BRINK: You're not very polite.

PUD: I'm politer than you, you big squashapussosha-puss.

BRINK: I'm afraid I never heard that word before.

PUD: Neither did I.

BRINK: You can make up words?

PUD: Sure, I can do anything?

BRINK: No, you can't. You can't even climb a tree.

PUD: I can too. I climbed that tree before you got up it and I climbed down again. That's more than you can do.

BRINK: You're right about that. But you couldn't do it now. Why, you can't even climb that fence.

PUD: I could do it with one hand.

BRINK: Let's see you.

PUD [*crosses to fence left*]: All right.
[*He goes to fence and tries and fails.*]

BRINK: You'll never get up on that side. Better come over to this side. It's much easier.
[PUD *does better but still slides back.*]

PUD: Ouch, that hurts my hand. Guess I'll have to get myself a heap o' tape.
[*Turns and crosses to screen door, quickly.*]

BRINK: Baby calf! Baby calf!

PUD [*turns to* BRINK]: Who's a baby calf!
[*He crosses to fence determinedly. He climbs and slowly approaches the cross beam.*]

BRINK: That's right. I never thought you could do it. I guess you must be stronger than I thought. Come on now. Just a little more. *Go along the edge there.* Get one leg over. There! That's it. Now you're here. Splendid! I guess you can do everything.

PUD: Golly, I can see far up here.

BRINK: Can you see me now?

PUD: Yes. Gee, why do you make your voice so whispery, Mr. Brink?

BRINK: Don't you like it?

PUD: Yes.

BRINK: Good. Can you see me?

PUD: Yes, I can see you. I'm up as high as you are now.

BRINK: Look at me!

PUD: Gee, you've got funny eyes, Mr. Brink. They make me dizzy. You've got ghost eyes.
[*Slowly* PUD *stands up, gripping the post.*]

BRINK: Look at me again. [PUD *does so.*] That's right.

Keep on looking at me. Give me your hand. Lean forward.

[PUD *suddenly loses his balance and falls.*]

PUD [*in terror*]: Gramps! Gramps! Gramps!

CURTAIN

SCENE VI

The tree. Later that night. Moonlight.

AT RISE: GRAMPS *is holding* PUD *in his arms. Walks toward tree.* BRINK *is visible.*

PUD: Gramps, I want a heap o' tape, my back hurts, my back.

GRAMPS: Hush, boy, hush for a minute. . . . Mr. Brink?

BRINK: Yes?

GRAMPS: Pud's in terrible pain. Doctor Evans just left and says he'll never be able to walk again. Why did you let him do it, Mr. Brink?

BRINK: My dear man, I didn't mean to hurt the boy. I just meant to take him. It was the only way out. I even waited a day to let the others force you. But you were too clever for them.

GRAMPS: But you could have found some other way than to pick on the boy.

BRINK: It is only through the boy that I have any hope

of getting down from here. He is the only reason that you won't let me come down. What if I should tell you that I'm bound to stay out the time to which you sentenced me? Until Miss Riffle dies?

GRAMPS: You're not, are you? You're not. You don't have to stay up there, do you?

BRINK: No. But I want you to understand how much it means to you, to your whole world, to deny me. Already the world is beginning to feel the pain and sorrow and bewilderment in keeping me here. It is getting worse every hour.

GRAMPS: I guess I tried to bite off more'n I could chew.

BRINK: Much more.

GRAMPS: Will you come down, please, and take us both?

BRINK: Gladly.

GRAMPS: Please come then. Quickly.

PUD: Gramps—

GRAMPS: Yes, boy.

PUD: A heap o' tape. My back hurts so awful—

GRAMPS: Yes, boy. There, there, boy. Just a minute— just a minute.

[BRINK *is down.* GRAMPS *holds out* PUD.]

BRINK: No, you are first. [*He touches* GRAMPS' *brow.* GRAMPS *suddenly straightens up.*] Ah, that's better, isn't it?

GRAMPS: Well, well. He was quite a load before. He's light as a feather now. Here, here.

[BRINK *bends over and touches* PUD. GRAMPS *lets*

PUD *down.* BRINK *and* GRAMPS *bend down to him.*]

PUD [*rousing*]: Hello, Mr. Brink.

BRINK: Hello, Pud.

PUD: Are we deaded, Gramps?

GRAMPS: Must be. I feel like a two-year-old. How do you feel?

PUD: I feel like a two-year-old, too, Gramps.

GRAMPS: Mr. Brink, why didn't you tell me it was goin' to be like this?

BRINK: My dear man, I've been trying to tell you how pleasant it is to go with me, but you wouldn't listen.

PUD: You talk so funny, Mr. Brink.

BRINK: Well, never mind me— Come on. Come along!

PUD [*crosses center,* GRAMPS *follows*]: But, where we goin', Gramps?

GRAMPS [*stops*]: Oh, yes—by golly, that's important. Where are we goin', Mr. Brink?

BRINK: You'll find out.

PUD [*looks at* BRINK]: How long will we be there?

BRINK: For eternity.

PUD [*looks at* GRAMPS]: How long is eternity, Gramps?

GRAMPS: Right smart piece of time, boy.

PUD: Anyway, we'll be there together, won't we, Gramps?

GRAMPS [*shaking hands with* PUD]: You're damn right we will be! You're damn right!

GRANNY [*off stage*]: Juleyun! Juleyun, do you have to use such language in front of the boy?

[*They all look up.*]

GRAMPS: Oh, hell, I thought you said she'd changed! [BRINK *shakes his head disapprovingly.* GRAMPS *throws* GRANNY *a kiss.* GRAMPS *and* PUD *march hand in hand through the gates and up the ramps.*]

CURTAIN

A NOTE ON THE TYPE IN WHICH
THIS BOOK IS SET

This book was set on the Linotype in Janson, a recutting made direct from the type cast from matrices (now in possession of the Stempel foundry, Frankfurt am Main) made by Anton Janson some time between 1660 and 1687.

Of Janson's origin nothing is known. He may have been a relative of Justus Janson, a printer of Danish birth who practised in Leipzig from 1614 to 1635. Some time between 1657 and 1668 Anton Janson, a punch-cutter and type-founder, bought from the Leipzig printer Johann Erich Hahn the type-foundry which had formerly been a part of the printing house of M. Friedrich Lankisch. Janson's types were first shown in a specimen sheet issued at Leipzig about 1675. Janson's successor, and perhaps his son-in-law, Johann Karl Edling, issued a specimen sheet of Janson types in 1689. His heirs sold the Janson matrices in Holland to Wolffgang Dietrich Erhardt, of Leipzig.

COMPOSED, PRINTED, AND BOUND BY VAIL-BALLOU PRESS, INC., BINGHAMTON, N. Y. PAPER MADE BY S. D. WARREN CO., BOSTON